Banking The Guy

The Lady's Manual To Captivating And Keeping Him Like No Other

J. S. PARKER

Copyright © 2016 J. S. Parker
All rights reserved.

DEDICATION

This Book Is Dedicated To All The Beautiful and Incredible Women Who Wants To Get The Guy, Keep Him, And Have An Exciting Relationship With The Man Of Their Dreams.

J.

CONTENTS

5 Keys to a man's heart

1	Introduction	1
2	Chapter 1: Why Do You Need These Secret Keys?	2
3	Chapter 2: Secret Key 1 - Desire	6
4	Chapter 3: Secret Key 2 - Feeling of Security	24
5	Chapter 4: Secret Key 3 - Respect and Compassion	31
6	Chapter 5: Secret Key 4 - Confidence	43
7	Chapter 6: Secret Key 5 – Give and Take the Lead	50
8	Section 2 Table of Contents	57
9	Section 3 Table of Contents	137
10	Conclusion: You've Reached Your Peak!	213

J.

ACKNOWLEDGMENTS

Introduction

Hello there, and thank you for purchasing this book. In the pages you are about to read, which totals 3 books in 1 package, you will find ways to captivate a man and his utmost attention, the ways to keep him wanting you more in the bedroom, as well as a bonus for soon-to-be or already married couples who want to have a lasting relationship with their spouse. The last book is included as a gift for you in preparation for your future marriage or even a long lasting intimate relationship if you do not plan to get married. This book will help you ladies on your journey to banking the guy and having a spicy and blissful relationship to come. I hope you enjoy this book, and find it informational.

Chapter 1

Why Do you need these secret keys?

Do you have a hard time connecting with men to even begin a relationship let alone take it to the highest level possible? Many people do, and that is because they do not know about the first thing about what it takes to capture a guy's attention and ultimately, his heart.

It is essential to unlock a man's heart, otherwise, you will not be able to know him as well as you wish you could, and the distance will make it hard to connect. A connection is important when in a relationship, as it is what determines the amount of passion you have years down the road. A weak connection makes for weak passion and limited intimacy once the honeymoon phase is over.

If you do not have passion and intimacy in a marriage, this can be a major problem, as they are what keep the love alive, and the marriage interesting. Without any interest in your marriage, it can cause many problems, including divorce, and infidelity.

So to avoid these issues you must learn about the secret keys, for without them you will be destined to have an average relationship, rather than a superb relationship. Which an average one can last forever, but a superb relationship will most definitely last forever.

Only about twenty percent of people know about these keys to a man's heart. They are the couples that you see that are eighty years old and still acting like young lovers. They are the couples that everyone aspires to be. These people are the happiest couples alive because they learned the secret keys to marriage, and to unlock their man's heart.

Why it is Pertinent to Know these Keys

These keys are the basis of obtaining a strong and intimate relationship. Almost everyone's goal in life is to get married, and have that marriage last forever. They want to be the couple that everyone looks up to, and that everyone comes to for advice. That is where these keys come in. They are designed to help you achieve that level of a relationship in your life. These are from a man's perspective, to help you understand more what they really want. Not what women say they want.

A man's heart is unique. It is unlike a woman's heart in many ways, and should be treated as such. You should want to know exactly how to open his heart to show you exactly how he wants to be loved.

Men are also stubborn at times. You may have already won his heart, but he has put up walls to try to prevent himself from falling. You have to break through these walls as well, which if you use these keys, should be easier than just whacking away at it with charm. Read on to find these keys.

CHAPTER 2:

SECRET KEY #1

Desire

Men do not say this aloud, which is why this key is such a big secret, but men love romance. They want their partners to put in a little romantic effort as well. This key is important, as without it, a man cannot be sure if you are really down for him or not. If he doesn't feel like you desire him, he will not completely open up to you. Very few couples realize how important this is, and that is why often times, you see relationships fizzle out so fast. Follow this key to strengthen your bond with the male species.

Romance

Describe your most romantic fantasy. Is it elaborate? Or simple? Either way, you most likely still have one. So does he. Men are romantic creatures by nature, but they also like to be romanced. Take him out to dinner, and pick up the check. Take him out to the movies, and pay for him.

Return the favor he probably often shows you quite frequently.

It doesn't even have to be that expensive either. When he has a long day at work, surprise him with his favorite dinner served by candlelight. In his day off, pack a picnic lunch, and drive to his favorite spot and enjoy a picnic. It doesn't have to always be fancy, you just need to put in as much effort into showing him you want him, as he does for you.

It is about feeling wanted, and loved. If you aren't putting in an effort to show him how much you care, how is he going to know that you are going to be there in the long run? He will feel like you are only there for what he can do for you, not what you can do together, and he will begin to feel used. Value a man. Don't expect to get treated like royalty if you are only going to treat him like a peasant.

To understand more about being romantic for a guy, this scenario will help you to understand more, that it isn't always about the big things, sometimes even the smallest gesture means the world to a guy.

Scenario

James looked over at his girlfriend, and wondered if she truly loved him. She said it all the time, but how did he know for sure? Was she just fronting to get his money or was she truly his ride or die chick? How could he be sure that she really loved him?

"Babe?" He called over to MaryBeth

"Yes, baby?" She replied

"Answer three questions for me. What is my favorite color? What was my favorite memory as a child? What is my favorite food?" James needed to know if she loved him as much as he loved her. He knew that her favorite color was purple, because it reminded her of the twilight hours when everything is quiet and still. He knew that her favorite childhood memory was when her dad took some free bikes and pieced them together to make her very first bike because they were too poor to buy a new one. He knew that her favorite food was Italian, and that it only became so when she met him, because he was Italian, and showed her how real cuisine was created, rather than restaurants that order frozen food and heat it up in a microwave. He wanted to see if she knew the answers to those questions.

"You don't have a favorite color, per say. You are color blind. You say that your favorite color would be emerald green because that is the color I told you my eyes were. Your favorite childhood memory was when you and your brother climbed the big oak tree in your backyard together, and talked about life and what your plans were for your futures. You said that was the first time you two had really ever bonded, and that was when you realized you wanted to be a real estate investor. You were nine. Your favorite food is Chinese, because it reminds you of when your mother used to take you to a Chinese restaurant every Friday for mother-son bonding time. The last time you did that with her was two days before she died. You used to dislike Chinese food, but went because she loved it, but after she died, the memories made you love it." She answered. "Now tell me. What is this about?"

"I was wondering if you loved me. No girl has ever paid enough attention to me, and focused mainly on my wallet. You answered every question perfectly. The first one to ever do so. I love you so much."

"How could you doubt I love you, James? I may not have a lot of money, but I try to show you every day that I love you. You should think about that, rather than focusing on little questions that anyone who pays attention to you could answer." MaryBeth replied, slightly offended that he felt she didn't love him.

As she walked out of the room, James sat and thought about what she said. He thought back over the course of their relationship, and thought about all the things she did for him regularly.

She cooks me dinner on a regular basis. When I have had a hard day, she rubs my back. Even though she is on her feet for over eight hours a day, and mine is just stress of a tenant not wanting to pay rent. She shows up on my longer days with my favorite meal, and we eat it together before we have to go back to work. For no reason at all, she told me to get in the car, and we drove to our favorite spot with some fast food, and ate while watching the trains pull into the station.

She always tells me she loves me before she goes to bed, even if she is angry with me. She never fails to ask me how my day was, and truly listen to the answer. Even though sometimes I tune her out when she talks about hers. I don't know what her favorite song is, or when her first heartbreak happened, but she sure as hell know mine. What have I done for her? I know the answer to three questions that anyone with half a brain could answer, and I buy her stuff. I take her out to fancy dinners, and spend money on her but that is about it, and yet she never questions my love for her. I want to marry this woman. She is my everything. She has a piece of me that no one else ever will. She truly has my heart.

James walked back into the bedroom, where he found MaryBeth crying. He sat beside her, and began to rub her back.

"I'm sorry. I am so sorry I ever doubted your love for me. I know I could say that every other girlfriend has only wanted my money, and it broke me, but in truth; I am just an ass. I love you, MaryBeth. I want to marry you someday. Not today, we still have a lot of things to work through, but if you forgive me, I promise that one day you will have an engagement ring on your finger." James said, pulling out a little ring and sliding it on her ring finger. "Do you accept my promise?"

"Yes. I forgive you as well." MaryBeth said, beaming with happiness while her eyes were still brimming with tears.

Discussion

James didn't realize until it was brought to his attention, all the little things that MaryBeth does for him to show her love. Sometimes you do have to give him a little wake up call to show him that you do play the romance card on a regular basis. Maybe do a big gesture here and there to really show him you care. But sometimes it just takes you telling him to think that gets his brain in gear. Be romantic, and even if he doesn't realize it at first, he will start to see all the little things you do for him, even when he doesn't notice you doing them.

Desire

You have to ignite a white-hot passion in him that makes him want to take you right here and right now almost any where you go. This desire is what fuels the passion in your relationship. If there is no passion, things get stale, and that is when people drift apart the most. If the bedroom isn't rocking, you better get packing, because you need a good sex life, and desire filled relationship to last for a long time.

How do you ignite this desire in him? It is simple. You have to desire him as well. Men are easily enticed, if you are willing to tap into your animalistic nature. You have to want to make him desire you, so that means you will have to be pro-active in your sexuality, and prove your prowess in the bedroom, along with outside the bedroom.

How is this done exactly? Ditch the missionary position. This is the bane of all sexual existence. There are so many more positions out there, where you don't have to lie there like a lifeless doll and take what he is giving you. (Ditch standard doggy style for gay couples. This is the missionary in the gay world.) Look up new positions and try them for yourselves. Try different styles. There are some that can spice up the bedroom if you are both willing to try it.

- BDSM: This is a type of sexual style that requires one partner to be dominant, and one partner to be submissive. Start out slow. Don't go "Fifty Shades of Grey" level the first day. Ease into it. Find out the limitations your bodies can handle, how tight you like the collars and ties, what you absolutely do not like, and so on and so forth. Knowing what you like is important, as if you don't like it, the experience will not be fun. Both of you have to be vocal if you want to know what each other likes and don't like. Also, come up with a safe word to use, so in the heat of the moment, you don't hurt yourselves.

- Roleplay: This is one for when you want to experience what it is like to have sex with someone different, yet still wanting that sex to be with your partner. You get little costumes, and you dress up as someone else. While dressed up as another person, you literally become that person. You are not yourself, you are a whole other person. This could mean you have your guy become the cable guy, or you become his secretary. There are many other people you can take on the role of, such as famous people, or make up your own personas. If you do not feel comfortable with role play, but are still intrigued by it, try it on a small scale. Have him be a fake person you make up, and vice versa. This will get you more comfortable with the idea, so you can more enjoy it.
- Making a Home Video: This can be a very good

bonding experience in the bedroom, as you can watch back the video you make, and see how much you were enjoying the sex. Once you both realize how good things are in the bedroom, you will never want to leave. Relax and enjoy it, though. Don't try to put on a show just because you are being filmed. You aren't a porn star, and neither is he. Just enjoy it. You can also see what positions work for you, and what doesn't when you play the video back. These videos should never be put on the internet, or used for any other reason than your viewing pleasure. If handled correctly, they can make for great material to get you in the mood as well.

- Watch Porn Together: This can give you an idea on positions to try, and also get you in the mood to do the deed. Find a video that you both like, and settle in. You can also try a bit of self stimulation while watching the video, but be careful not to distract yourself, or your partner from the video itself. The whole point is to learn new positions and bond. Remember though, porn is an act. Do not expect to have super explosive orgasms the first time you try a position. You most likely will have to practice a few times for it to even feel good.

- There are many ways to spark up some interest in the bedroom, but how do you make him want to do these things? How do you spark the carnal desire in him? How do you show him you want him so bad it makes your stomach do flips? There are a few ways that are fool proof.
- Send Him Little Notes: You can leave sticky notes all over the house for him, in his car, in his lunchbox if he has one. You can also text him all the things you would like to do to him.

Tell him that you aren't wearing any underwear or something like that. Give him something to want later that night.

- Tease Him: Kiss him seductively in the hall way and then keep moving along. Rub your rear against his junk, and then walk away. Play footsie with him when you eat dinner. Make him desire you, turn him on, but then leave him hanging. At the end of the night he will want you so bad, he will do anything to have you.

- Be Playful: Sometimes the biggest turn on is when you act like a kid. Being free-spirited can be the biggest turn on for guys, because they like knowing you are happy and having fun. Tickle him, and then make him chase you to the bedroom and tackle you on the bed. Play wrestle a little bit, and watch the playing turn into sex real fast. Sometimes the best foreplay, is to simply play.

- You have to create a white-hot desire in the pit of his stomach, one that makes him crave you when you are away, and not want to leave your side when you are near. You have to make him think about you constantly, to the point where he doesn't even want you to go to the restroom because that means being away from you for too long.

- This desire will unlock the part of his heart that makes him want to commit. He won't want to leave, because he is too devoted to you, and he loves you way too much to walk away from everything you have together. You have to keep this desire alive, and strong, to keep the relationship strong and healthy.

- Here is a scenario that should help you get a mental picture of what that desire looks like. Caution. This one is mildly graphic, but if you are an adult reading this, as the disclaimer warns, you have probably read much worse.

- **Scenario**

- *He wanted her. He wanted her more than he has ever wanted anyone. The way she teased him drove him insane. It was like she took pleasure in keeping him aroused to the point of pain. She would pay for it, when she finally let him have her.* These thoughts swirled around Mason's brain, and left him winded. He thought back to when they first met.

- Lacy wasn't like a lot of girls. That is what attracted Mason to her. He was tired of girls throwing themselves at him. He was tired of girls who had nothing more to offer than a loose vagina, and some amateur head. These women bored Mason, so he never kept them around much longer than a night. Lacy, however, showed very little interest in Mason when they first met. She looked him up and down, offered her hand in a professional manner, and said it was nice to meet him. Like she was at a job interview. She didn't blush, or swoon, or make any indication that she found Mason attractive. He had to have her. She was exactly what he wanted. A challenging woman.

- He became more and more infatuated with her as the night drew on, and he listened to her talk, and engaged in conversation with her. She was Harvard educated, and it showed. She wasn't haughty or anything, really she was very humble, but when she spoke her words were eloquent and well thought out. She didn't use 'like' in between every word, as most girls tend to do. Instead, every word out of her mouth was carefully planted like she was speaking a puzzle.

- She turned him on. Plain, and simple. He had to have a date with her.
- "Excuse me, Lacy? I am enamored by your eloquence, and would love to talk to you more, one-on-one. Would you care to have a cup of coffee with me after this party is over?" Mason asked
- "Why don't we leave right now? I feel I am boring everyone else." Lacy said
- "I highly doubt you are boring anyone, but if you wish, I would love to go at once."
- They left the club, and walked down the street to a little coffee shop that was open twenty four hours a day. This was one of Mason's spots to think, and he wanted Lacy to experience it as well. When they walked in, he could tell that she was star-struck with the place. It wasn't well known, but it was cozy. He offered to buy her coffee, but she refused,

stating that she was glad to have an excuse to leave the club.

- "I hope you don't think that I am like other girls, Mason." Lacy said as soon as the found a cozy nook to sit down.
- "I beg you are pardon?" Mason nearly choked on his latte
- "I don't put out on the first date. You have to win my heart. You can't just bring me to a quaint little coffee shop, and expect me to sleep with you tonight." Lacy was blunt with what she spoke, there was no beating around the bush.
- "Of course I don't think you are like other girls. In fact, I have never brought a woman here before."
- As if on cue, the shop owner came out then to greet Mason.
- "Mason, my old friend. Are you enjoying your

evening? Oh! You have a lady with you! Forgive me for interrupting, I have never seen this before. Enjoy yourselves." The shop owner ducked back into his office with a bright red face.

- "Well I guess I don't need to ask you to prove that you have never brought a woman here."
- They sat and talked the night away. In the wee hours of the morning, Mason drove Lacy home, as her friends had already left the club.
- "Lacy, can I see you again?" Mason asked, as she stepped out of the car.
- "I would like that very much."
- Three months later, Lacy practically lived with him. They often slept in the same bed. And he still had not been able to make love to her. That is what he wanted. He didn't want to just have sex with her, he wanted to make love to her.

- "What is on your mind, Mace?" Lacy asked, sitting on his lap.

- "I want you, Lacy. More than I have ever wanted anyone. I love you. I truly love you. I want to make passionate love to you, in a way no man ever has. I want to give you the world, if you will let me. You are the one I want. Forever."

- "Mason, that is what I have been wanting to hear since we met. Tonight you will finally get what you want. Me."

- That night was the most mind blowing night of Mason's life. Lacy felt perfect for him. They didn't leave the bedroom for hours. Everything was perfect.

- Flash forward two years later, and Lacy still teased him. He still wanted her as much as he did from day one. He couldn't imagine life with any other woman, as she was the only one who lit such a desire in him.

- **Discussion**
- Lacy made Mason desire her, by not always being readily available. She let him know she was into him, but she did not give up everything from the beginning, and even after she gave it all up, she still kept that playfulness up in the relationship, making him want her bad enough to always desire her.
- This is what you have to do in a relationship. You have to keep your partner interested in you. Don't think that just because you have been together for a long time, that means you have to act like an old couple. Be playful. Show each other how much you care.

-
-
-
-

CHAPTER 3

SECRET KEY #2

Make Him Feel Safe

- Men will never admit that they need to feel safe in a relationship. This key is a secret, because society makes men feel that they have to be macho all the time. This is the furthest from the truth, and you should not believe this, as everyone needs to feel safe. Not just physically, but emotionally.

- Couples that know this often have less fights, and less time spent angry at each other. Fights and arguments do not stem from someone doing something that you don't agree with, they stem from being afraid that they are going to leave you. You get angry because you don't feel safe, and you are scared you are going to be left alone, so you throw up a wall. Men do the same thing as everyone else. Only they will never admit that is why they have a wall up.

- You have to make him want to take all of his walls down and be open with you. Make him feel like you want to know everything about him. Not just where he grew up, what his favorite color is, and what music does he like. Ask him if he ever sucked his thumb, did he have a teddy bear or a blankie? What was his favorite television show growing up? Has he ever been in trouble? What are his aspirations, and fears? Ask him about his nightmares. Do not be satisfied with one word answers. Give him information about you every time he divulges something about himself.

- **Emotional Safety**
- You have to be his safety net as he is free-falling into love with you, just as he has to be yours. You have to catch each other, and you can't fall if you don't trust the other person with your heart. Be open always. You can't expect him to open up to you when you won't open up to him. It is a give and take relationship, when you want to unlock the part of his heart he holds dearest to him.
- To make him feel emotionally safe, you have to let him know that you won't let him down. This often means listening to him talk about things you aren't necessarily interested in.
- A man has to be able to cry around you to feel truly and completely safe in a relationship. Sometimes you have to assure him that it is

okay to cry. Hold him when you see him having a weak moment, and let him know that sometimes even the strongest mountain breaks down. If he can't cry around you, he won't be truly open to you. Men are at their most vulnerable moments in life when they break down in front of someone, because they are bred to believe that crying means you are weak. So if a man finally cries in front of you, you have won his heart.

- Here is a scenario of how to know if you make him feel emotionally safe.
- **Scenario**
- Josh loved his boyfriend very much, but he felt as if Alex was still closed off. Josh was definitely the more feminine of the two, so he was very open with Alex. Alex however, often changed the subject when it came to his past. Josh knew that Alex loved him, he just wasn't

ready to completely open up. Josh was understanding, and never pushed, but still let his love know that he was there for him.

- One day, Alex came home in a horrible mood. Josh didn't know what was wrong, but he ran up and hugged Alex anyway.
- "Oh, baby, I can just tell you had a horrible day. Would you like to talk about it?" Josh asked.
- "Actually I would like that very much, babe." Alex said with a tight throat.
- "Come sit down darling, let me make you your favorite tea while you compose your thoughts."
- Josh hurried off to the kitchen, while Alex sat down on the couch, looking lost and forlorn. Josh's hear broke just looking at how sad his love looked. After the tea finished brewing, Josh hurried back into the living room, and

handed Alex his tea, made just the way he liked it.

- "What happened love?" Josh asked gently.
- "I guess there is no sense in beating around the bush. My brother is dead. He was shot in the head last night in a drug deal gone wrong." Alex said
- "I am so sorry love. I didn't know you had a brother, but I am heartbroken for you nonetheless." Josh said, wrapping his arms around Alex.
- "I didn't talk about him much because I was ashamed of him. He was a drug addict. He was always asking when he could meet you, and I always made excuses. I feel horrible now, because he was the only one who supported me when I came out as gay. My parents kicked me out, and he gave me a place to stay. He was the only family I had,

and I judged him for something he had about as much control over as I do being gay." Alex broke down in tears.

- Josh sat there and held Alex, his heart breaking for him, as it also beamed with love, because Alex was finally opening up to him. He was sad that Alex's only true family was dead, but happy that Alex trusted him enough to tell him everything. His heart swelled with love for the man in his arms crying his eyes out.

- **Discussion**

- Alex was very closed off when it came to talking about his past, because it hurt to much to talk about, and he didn't want to cry in front of Josh, and Josh felt distanced from Alex due to his wall he threw up. Once Alex finally started talking about himself, Josh knew that Alex truly loved him, and that he trusted him finally. This gave Josh a happy feeling, even in the midst of a sad time, which allowed him to truly comfort Alex in his moment of need.

- **Why Do You Need This Key Again?**
- This key is essential in opening up an intense bond between you and your partner. When you feel comfortable enough to be completely open with each other, you learn more about the other than you could ever imagine. This is important, because to truly love someone, you have to truly know them. Once you truly know everything about someone, loving them becomes a whole lot easier.

-
-
-
-
-
-
-
-
-
-
-
-
-
-
-

-

-

-

CHAPTER 4:

SECRET KEY #3

Respect and Compassion

- What is the one thing that anyone wants more than anything in the world? That is right, respect. Respect is rated the number one thing that a person wants in life. It is even more of a priority than love, because you can't have love if you don't have respect.
- Respect is what makes the world go round. Think Aretha Franklin. R-E-S-P-E-C-T. This song is about how just a little respect can make a world of difference. You have to

respect your partner not only as your partner, but as a human being as well. You can't expect them to be perfect, and you have to respect that sometimes they have to make mistakes.

- This is where compassion comes in. When your partner makes a mistake, it is always important to show them compassion and understanding. This way they know that you care enough to help them make it through the mistakes they have made.
- **Why is this a Secret Key?**
- Most people do not know that men need more respect and compassion in the relationship. Men are often more insecure then women, they are just better at hiding it. Respect and compassion assure him that you love him and care about him, and that he is good enough for you. If he feels that he is worthy of you, he

will become the most devoted person you have ever met. This key unlocks the section in his heart tied to fidelity. If he feels worthy of you, he will do anything to stay there. If he does not feel worthy of you, he will look for someone who makes him feel worthy.

- **_EGO_**
- This all boils down to ego. A man's ego is a powerful thing. Sometimes, if not treated properly, he can become borderline narcissistic. If he feels that he is not getting the respect he deserves, he will look to get it in any way he can. This is where a lot of severe relationship problems stem from. Emotional abuse, physical abuse, infidelity. This is all a problem created when a man is beaten down. Not necessarily by you, but by the world. This is what causes people to split up, and can ruin what seemed to be a perfect

relationship.

- Men aren't always aware of their ego issues, so they can't tell you what they need. That is not to excuse a man who becomes abusive or a cheater, or even to say that a man is helpless. They know right from wrong, they just don't realize what is causing them to do wrong. If he is abusive or a cheater, then you should leave. No questions asked. Leave. However, if he is just being angry for no reason, maybe you aren't showing each other enough respect and compassion.
- **How to Show Him Respect**
- Be there for him: If he has a gig, or something important, go with him. Even if you aren't interested. Being there for him, and respecting him enough to support him shows him how much you care. If he needs you to listen to him, do so. Let him rant on about something

you don't care about, but pay attention. Just because you don't care doesn't give you a free pass to ignore him or tune him out.

- Respect His Privacy: Trust is a big thing in a relationship. Both parties need their privacy on some things, and breaking that privacy is saying that you don't trust your partner enough to give him space. A big thing that a lot of women do is go through his phone. If you can't trust him enough to leave his phone alone, you probably shouldn't be in a relationship. You also shouldn't snoop through his drawers or his personal things. Let him have his privacy, just as you want yours.

- Respect His Personal Space: You don't have to be together every free moment you both have. Sometimes, spending time apart when you have free time is a good thing. You can do your own thing, and don't have to worry about if the other person is having fun. Men need this personal space to unwind after a hard day. Women do as well, but we are focusing on men here. If he doesn't text you back immediately, he is probably in the shower or taking a nice hot bubble bath. It does NOT mean he is cheating on you. Let him have his space without worrying about him stepping out on you. If you trust and respect him, he most likely will not want to do anything to break that trust. But if you don't trust him, he might just give you a reason not to.

- Respect the Fact that He is Human: Men are not robots, and they are not slaves. He has needs, and he needs them tended to at times as well. You cannot expect him to wait on you hand and foot, yet not turn around to do the same for him. Also he will mess up. Don't hang it over his head for the rest of his life.

Get through it, and then get over it.

- Those are some ways that you can show that you respect him. Men are easy to please, and as they do not have the hormone fluxes that women do, it is more straightforward, but you still have to dig a little to find out his needs. He will give you what you need, if you respect him enough to let him.

- **Compassion**

- Compassion is important for when he is having a hard day or makes a mistake. You have to be willing to be compassionate towards someone to ever make a relationship work. Compassion is the difference between healing his heart and breaking it. If you are compassionate, he will trust you with things he doesn't trust anyone else with.

- **How to Be Compassionate**

- Take Care of Him: If he is having a bad day,

cook for him. Clean for him. Rub his back and cuddle him. I know this new-age mentality is that women are not a man's slave and that he can do for himself. That may be true, but sometimes you have to take care of him. In return, he will take care of you.

- Be Understanding: Men are human, and they will mess up. Don't overreact if he buys they wrong type of toilet paper, or the wrong grade of milk. They don't always get everything right. You have probably messed up sometimes as well. Did he freak out over the little things? Relax. If he isn't out killing people, or cheating on you, then discuss it calmly on why you prefer things a different way, and then make like Elsa and 'Let it Go'.
- Don't Ridicule Him: If he is not as advanced as you in some areas, do not make him feel bad for it. If you can read the best, and he can do

math the best, combine your strengths. Don't make him feel like less of a person because he can't do what you can. Don't tell him he needs to get better. If he wants to, then help him, but don't tell him he has to.

- Listen to His Problems: The best thing you can ever do is just listen when he wants to talk. Not only will you learn some new things, but you will show him that you are invested in him, and by showing him a little compassion, you make him feel like he is important.
- This scenario will show you how respect and compassion can help save a relationship.
- **Scenario**
- Rachel was worried about Rick. He had been acting distant lately, and was gone a lot. He always hid his phone and wouldn't let her touch it. Everyone said that he was probably cheating, but she trusted him to have a good

reason for all of these things. She didn't want to be let down again by another man.

- *I will have a talk with him when he gets home tonight. I will ask him why he has been acting this way.*
- Suddenly she heard a phone ring. She checked her pockets, but it wasn't hers. She investigated the sound, and found her boyfriend's phone behind the toilet. There was a strange number calling.
- *Should I answer it? No. I trust him. It is probably just a telemarketer, and his phone probably fell behind the toilet this morning, and he didn't grab it cause he was running late to work.*
- Rachel knew that Rick would be home in a few hours, so she busied herself with errands and cleaning the house up. Five o'clock rolled by, and Rick still wasn't home. She started to get

worried, and with no way to contact him, she couldn't allay her fears. But she told herself to remain calm, and that he would show up.

- Finally, around seven o'clock, Rick came walking in the door. Rachel flung herself into his arms because she was so worried. Then she noticed that he didn't smell like the fiberglass mill, and he was surprisingly clean for being at work all day.
- "Rick. We really need to talk." Rachel whispered, on the verge of tears.
- "What's wrong?" Rick asked her
- "I have been trusting of you, and I still trust you to tell me what is going on. I am trying not to assume you are cheating. However it is really hard to think of any other explanation why you have been coming home late, hiding your phone behind the toilet and getting strange calls. I didn't answer it by the way.

Your clothes are too clean to be coming out of the fiberglass company, and they are the same clothes you walked out of here wearing. You don't smell like you normally do after work. Please just tell me what is going on." Rachel burst into tears.

- "Oh Rach." Rick sighed, pulling her into his arms. "I got laid off a couple of weeks ago, and have been looking for a job ever since. That number was probably a job calling so I have to call back tomorrow. I'm late because I have been doing odd jobs to continue making enough money to support us, so you don't have to. I wanted to tell you, I just didn't want you to worry."

- "That is what this is all about? You knew I was cheated on several times by my last guy, and you leave me worrying that it is happening again? Babe, I would have understood if you had told me, and I would have supported you, and even got a job myself if need be. I love you, and I want you to tell me about your problems. Please don't hide something like this again."

- "Oh Rachel, I love you so much, and I didn't realize how bad it looked. I am so sorry, and I promise to always tell you about these things from now on." Rick said, kissing Rachel passionately.

- **Discussion**

- Rachel could have jumped to conclusions and accused Rick of cheating on her, thus making him angry for her not trusting him. However, she decided to ask him about it and listen to what he had to say. She was understanding when he told her what was going on, and let him know she wanted him to bring his troubles to her, even if it meant that he had to put some stress on her. She wanted to take on these problems together.

- By being compassionate, and respecting him enough to trust him, she avoided what could have been a really big fight. Instead they were brought closer together, as they opened up with what was bothering them.
- **Why is this Key Important Again?**
- You have to respect each other to get anywhere in a relationship. Without respect you have nothing, and you can't truly love someone if you do not respect them. Compassion is needed to ensure that your relationship is not a miserable one. You have to respond with compassion to avoid having an argument blown out of proportion. People are not robots or dolls, they will mess up.
- You have to use this key to unlock the part of a man's heart that trusts you. He doesn't open it

up for just anyone. Most men do not trust half of the people they say are close to them. They could not be vulnerable to these people. You have to unlock that for yourself.

•

•
•
•
•
•
•
•
•
•
•
•
•
•

CHAPTER 5:
SECRET KEY #4

- Be Confident

- Men do not want to be with a woman who is always questioning if she is good enough for him. They want a woman who knows her worth. Men want to know they are with someone who feels valued. If you aren't confident, it makes his job of making you feel secure that much harder. He feels he always has to lift your self esteem, and that can be a hard job for anyone.

- Confidence is not always just knowing you are worthy of love, however. It is also taking care of yourself. Taking care of your personal hygiene and keeping yourself groomed. You do not have to be perfect, just put an effort into keeping yourself clean and well kept.
- Most people don't realize that this is important in a relationship, and that is what makes it a secret key. It is important to use this to unlock his desires for you if you are looking to start a relationship with him, and you must remain confident and well kept to unlock his never waning desires for you.
- **Confidence**
- Everyone has their insecurities, there is no

doubt about that. However it is important to not let your insecurities rule your life. You can have some things that make you not so sure about yourself, but you have to be able to work through them.

- Confidence is important in any aspect of your life, but it is certainly important in relationships. Not only do you have to be confident in yourself, you have to be confident in your relationship as well. You can't expect a relationship to thrive if you don't have any confidence in it. You have to believe that it will succeed, and that you are good enough for it to succeed.
- In this scenario, you will learn more about what poor confidence can do to a relationship.
- **Scenario**
- Blake was super insecure. He constantly doubted himself, and if he was good enough

for his boyfriend Michael. Michael hated that Blake was so insecure, and wished he could see how gorgeous he was. It caused many fights, because Blake felt that he wasn't good enough and did everything in his power to make Michael see that. Which included picking fights for no reason at all.

- *I wish I was confident enough to make this relationship work. I am just not good enough for him. He is perfect, and I am a fat lard. I really need to lose weight. I am so fat. Why does he stay with me? Can't he see I'm a disaster?*

- These are the thoughts that went through Blake's head daily. He couldn't ever get close to Michael, because he was scared that Michael would see that he was a disaster. He constantly had a wall up that Michael was trying to break down.

- *I'm exhausted. Blake never lets me in, and I'm am so tired of trying to break through the walls he puts up. I wish he could see how much he means to me. He is perfect just the way he is, if only he would stop worrying so much.*

- Michael was tired of always trying to boost Blake's self esteem, so with a heavy heart, he broke up with Blake.

- "I told you I wasn't good enough!" Blake screamed, with tears in his eyes.

- "You imbecile! That is the reason I am breaking up with you! You don't feel like you are good enough for me, and I am tired of you ignoring every effort I make to try to show you otherwise! You are perfect just the way you are, and I wish I could have made you see that! I don't want to leave, but I can't keep breaking my heart when you won't let me into yours!" Michael yelled back.

- "So you aren't breaking up with me because I'm not breaking up with you, you are merely breaking up with me because I feel like I am not?" Blake whispered
- "Yes. I want nothing more than to be with you, but I have to think of my own emotional health as well."
- "What if I promised to get help for my insecurities? Would you stay with me? I love you Michael, I just don't want to be hurt anymore. I want you to love me too."
- "I do love you Blake, and if you actively get help, then yes, I will stay. But you have two weeks to show me you are trying." Michael said, embracing Blake.
- **Discussion**
- Blake's insecurities almost cost him the love of his life. He was so worried about Michael

pushing him away, that he didn't realize he was the one doing the pushing. Blake was not confident in himself, and it was tiresome for Michael to always be the one to supply the confidence for the both of them. Michael felt like Blake couldn't truly love him, because he never let him in. It almost destroyed their relationship beyond repair.

- If Blake had realized that Michael wanted to be with him for who he was, he would have avoided this whole scene, and been very happy. Let your confidence shine through. You may not feel confident, but fake it until you make it. If you seem confident, you will start to feel confident.

-

- **Take Care of Yourself**
- Men want women to be healthy. This does not mean that you have to eat organic food, and

wear full face makeup every day of your life. Just shower regularly, and keep yourself groomed. If you are a slob, and unhygienic, most men will feel that is a sign of lack of confidence, and they will stay away from you. You have to make yourself appear to be ready for a relationship to find the right relationship. If you look like you don't care about yourself you are going to attract someone who doesn't care about you as well.

- If you are in a relationship, and start letting yourself go, you will make your man feel like you don't care about the relationship as much as you used to. (This doesn't count if you have kids. Though you should still try to shower regularly) You should always want to keep your hygiene up regardless of your relationship status.
- **Why is this Key Important?**

- This key unlocks a man's desire for you. Human's primal instinct is to mate, and men are really close to their primal instincts. He will be looking for a strong woman suitable for carrying his children, so that his offspring are strong and successful. By being confident, and taking care of yourself, you attract men that will value you, and treat you well. If you are not confident, and do not take care of yourself, you often will attract losers and abusers.

  -
  -
  -
  -
  -
  -
  -
  -
  -

CHAPTER 6:

SECRET KEY #5

Give and Take on the Lead

This key is one of the most secret keys there are, because most people don't realize that the man doesn't always wear the pants in a relationship. You both have to make the big decisions together, and take turns on the smaller ones. You cannot let one single person take control of the relationship. If you work together, you unlock a bond that allows him to see you as an equal and not as below him.

- If you make all of the decisions in the relationship, you allow him to be passive, but if he makes all the decisions, you become passive. Neither one of you should become passive, because this is a one way ticket to a controlling relationship. While it does not always end up that way, fifty six percent of relationships where one person is in charge of most or all of the decisions turn into be abusive relationships.

- The solution to avoid this problem is to take turns making decisions. Even the smaller decisions like where to go when you go out to eat, or what to watch on television. On the

bigger decisions, make them together. Especially on whether or not to buy a house or start a family, or any big purchase.
- Also, take care of finances together, or split them up equally. You cannot give one person complete control of the finances, and expect to not have some control issues. Money is the biggest player in a controlling relationship. If one person has all the control of the money, they can tell the other partner what they can and cannot do, and once you get a taste of that power, it escalates from there.
- The best way to avoid this is to get a joint account if you are married that has both of your names on it, so you both can access the funds, or have separate accounts with only your name on it, so the other partner can't access the funds. If you do this though, you have to decide how to split the bills.

Otherwise, there will be issues with bills not getting paid, and utilities being shut off. This is if you live together. If not, you don't have to worry about it.

- If you don't want to take turns on even the little decisions, then work together to decide everything. From where you want to eat, to where you want to live. Working together will create a strong bond between you two as well. You will grow closer together as you achieve things together. Think about it. If you make great strides in your life with the one you love, who are you going to celebrate with? That's right, them. So it only makes sense that if you make all your decisions together, you will grow closer due to the fact that you celebrate every achievement as one. You have to want to work together though, otherwise, you will argue more than you work together.

-
-
- **Why is this Key Important?**
- You want to unlock his heart in a way that makes him see you as an equal rather than a lesser, as society tries to make everyone think. If he sees you as his equal, he will learn to depend on you, rather than walk all over you. There will be less debates on who should make what decisions, and who is always right, because you will both be able to compromise and work together to achieve a blissful relationship.

-
-
-
-
-
-

The Lady's Manual
(Section 2)

To Ignite The FIRE

In The Relationship With Your Man

•
•
•

- J. S. PARKER

CONTENTS

1	Introduction: Ignite Your Relationship	57
2	Chapter 1: Five Keys To FIRE Up Your Relationship	63
3	Chapter 2: Secret Key 1 – Making A Game-Time Decision	76
4	Chapter 3: Secret Key 2 – Know & Share Your Turn-Ons	89
5	Chapter 4: Secret Key 3 – Maintain The Mystery	102
6	Chapter 5: Secret Key 4 – Change It Up	115
7	Chapter 6: Secret Key 5 – Connecting On All Sexual Cylinders	124

- introduction
- ignite your relationship

Carol and Alex have been together for seven years now, and yet it feels like twenty. Their son is in kindergarten, and the baby is just at the age where she's getting into everything. Outside of his full-time job as a contractor, Alex acts as a handyman on the side in hopes of saving the down payment for a new home. Carol telecommutes from home so she can be there for the kids and avoid the high cost of daycare. Although Carol and Alex are emotionally bonded, their sex life leaves much to be desired—literally. What started out as "hot and heavy," is now a weekend quickie between HBO and streaming Facebook.

-

- Even though Alex and Carol agree their sexual relationship needs a reboot, they have no idea how to recapture their initial fire. They have managed to have sex a few times a month, but more times than not, it's more duty than dazzling. At first, they tried to reassure one another by promising sex tomorrow, when they'd had more sleep or when the kids went to grandmas. The problem was, tomorrow never came.

-

- What Carol and Alex need are some help

building a fire beneath their waning sexual relationship. At this point, it's going to take more than a match stroke over kindling to reeve up their sexual appetites. This one's going to need a "five-star" fire up—or should I say a "Five Key" fire up? Can you relate? Before you've finished reading about the "Five Keys," you and your partner will be sitting down this book and giving each one of them a try.

-

- Between these pages, we will present proven strategies and practices designed to get you an incredible sexual relationship with your partner. After reading this book, you'll be wanting more—sex, that is. These Five Keys will give you so much fire in your sex life that you'll soon burn through all those bad habits you've created and release your inner sexual beast.

-

- Oh, that got your attention, didn't it? If you found yourself shaking your head in agreement when hearing of the decrease in sexual appetite between Carol and Alex, you'll be encouraged to know that most all decreases or dysfunctions are fixable. Your sexual issues might be caused by completely different things, but the pain and hurt suffered from the lack of good sex are the same. These "Five Keys" will not only examine what could be causing your problems but will also give you practical "how to" steps to take you and your partner to a whole new sexual high. By believing in and embracing the Five Keys to light up your sexual experiences, you can expect...
- More intimacy in your relationship

- Better communication of your needs and wants
- Greater physical prowess
- Closer emotional connection
- More confidence and self-esteem
- Fewer suspicions and doubts regarding your partner
- More energy and sexual desire
- Better overall health and well-being
- Flat out—more hot sex

•

- These five powerful Keys to reigniting your sexual fires will teach you how to reset your sexual expectations. You'll begin to see yourself as a dynamic lover and nurturing partner. As we break down each Key element to reigniting your sexual fires, you'll discover more creative and mysterious ways to please your partner and yourself. They'll teach you how to build anticipation for your next sexual encounter. Who knows, you and your lover will probably adopt this as your next "in bed" read.

-

- Communication is everything, including how you speak with your body as well as your words. Powerful physical messages can be sent without ever saying a word. Like a moth to a flame, your partner will soon want to see what this new you is all about. As you learn more about yourself, you'll be able to more effectively communicate to your partner what to do to make you tremble with anticipation.

-

- Notice, so far, we've talked about "building" the fire. Like every fire, it begins with a spark of promise, interest, and curiosity. To build a true fire, that spark must be tended to, fanned, and heaped with materials to create a rising flame. If you fail to tend to the fire constantly, it goes out.

If you cover the fire with the sands of judgment, stress, doubt, and fear, your fire will be distinguished before it's had a chance to heat up your sex life.

-

- Before you know it, instead of giving a stranger that sexually charged look or experience that fiery glow from an eye-to-eye light from a passer-by, you'll be eagerly waiting in the bedroom for your lover to come to bed—if you make it to the bedroom. The Keys will provide playful and exciting ways to motivate yourself and your partner to engage in more creative sex. I'm not talking about the legs-over-your-head kind of sex unless of course, that's your turn-on. I'm talking about ways that engage your mind as well as your body. The Keys show you how to be fully committed—how to give sex the full- Monty treatment.

-
- From learning to please yourself to giving the "let's have hot sex" signal to your partner, discovering the importance of timing and mounting anticipation is crucial. There are perfect times to have sex, and then there are perfect times to have naughty sex. There are proper places to have sex, and then there are under-the-table places to share hidden sexual activities. Having fun and being creative is not an option; it's a necessity.
- So, are you "up" for this? You will be, especially when you learn these Five Keys and apply them to your sex life.

-
-
-
-
-

CHAPTER 1

five keys to fire up

Before presenting the Five Keys to ignite the fire in your relationship, we wanted you to know these statistics. Recent studies tell the real story: More than 1/3 of women between the ages of 18 to 59 years old suffer from a lack of desire for sex (1). Women are not the only ones experiencing problems in their sex lives. Sixty-two percent of men today say no to sex more frequently than women (2). We've lost our drive! It's not that most of can't enjoy sex or can't perform, it's that most of us just don't want to have sex. Perhaps the sex we've been having hasn't left us wanting more of the same.

-

- Of course, a decrease in your sex drive can be caused by a number of medical reasons, such as depression, high blood pressure, medications, increased stress hormones, and low testosterone levels, among other things. Or, decreased sex drives can be correlated to low energy levels, over-crowded schedules, family distractions, abusive backgrounds, or poor past experiences with sex. Some with medical issues or deep emotional scars may need to consult with a professional sex therapist or physician to regain healthy functioning.

-

- The first thing you need to do is know if you have a sexual problem. No, you don't have to go to a meeting, introduce yourself to the group, and tell them all about your sexual dysfunction. Although I'm sure there's an encounter group for that, as well. It might be less stressful and more enlightening to examine some of the things that could be causing your low libido. Keep in mind, the reasons for a decreased sex drive can be much different between men and women.

-

- **Why Is There No Fire in Your Relationship?**
- To many women, sex seems somewhat unimportant; you might say it's low on their "to-do" list. Women who display these rather lackluster emotions toward sex certainly don't flip the fire switch for their partners. Emotional

detachment to sex sucks all the energy out of the act. Many men who lack desire for sex can usually link their doused fire to job-related stress, money worries, and repeated rejection. Having sex then becomes robotic and routine; there just isn't enough return on the emotional or physical investment.

- Here are some of the most common reasons both men and women have given for decreases in their sexual desires.
- Fear of being judged or criticized
- No more emotional connection
- Just another chore
- Too many interruptions
- Too much on their mind
- Don't have the energy
- Resentment from sex being used as a commodity
- Not enough tenderness or intimacy
- Boring—they've done it all

- He/she takes me for granted
- No fun
- Feelings of unattractiveness
- They'd rather relax in front of the television
- Unsatisfied with physical appearance
- Painful
- Sex is perceived as wrong or sinful
- Previously abusive relationship
- No foreplay—just hop on, hop off, roll over
- Been too long and now they feel awkward
- Partner never initiates sex (3)
- The list of reasons for a decreased sex drive is infinite. Then there's the question of boring sex; you're having sex frequently, but it's not that hot, passionate sex that used to make you want to climb out of your skin. To some degree, that's to be expected. It's not that familiarity breeds contempt—it's more like regular sex with the same person can cause complacency. It's a

proven fact that people have an instinctive need for newness. We prefer new cars to ones that have given us great service. We want new clothes over those that are more comfortable. Deep within us, we fantasize about the excitement of new partners. Unfortunately, when a new partner is found, it isn't long before that same old bedfellow "boredom" comes to call.

- Some men and women are far too patient, putting up with little to no sex for years. What if it's too late to start a fire in your relationship? Put your mind to rest. It's never too late to become a more excitingly sexual person. Even if you cannot reignite the fire in this relationship, learning these Five Keys can help you to build within yourself, and that will certainly get your partner's attention. There is no list of signs that will tell you when your sex drive is waning—you are already experiencing the one most glaring sign—no sex.

-
- So, what are the Five Keys to reignite the fire in your relationship? We thought you'd never ask!
-
-
- **The Five Keys to Ignite the Fire in Your Relationship**
-
- We'll go into greater detail later, but for right now I'll introduce the keys and briefly describe their meaning.
-
- *Key #1: Making a Game-Time Decision*
- If you have known for a long time that your relationship was blowing a bit cold, you have a decision to make. Putting the fire back into a relationship doesn't just happen by accident. To create a fire from embers takes a conscious decision and firm resolve to make it happen.
- *Key #2: Know & Share Your Turn-ons*

- Many people don't know what really turns them on because they've never exposed themselves. Not that kind of expose! They've never explored their own bodies to understand what turns them on. Being familiar with your "boiling" points is important to know, and to share with your partner. It's especially important if your turn-ons are a bit out of the norm. We'll examine some of those in a later chapter.

-

- *Key #3: Maintain the Mystery*
- Part of that newness we spoke of earlier comes from the fact that a new partner holds mysteries that have yet to be unfolded. We haven't been privy to their private habits that can be a buzz kill to sexual desire. We don't know their secrets, but we look forward to uncovering each tantalizing detail. For this reason, you need to reserve some things for your mystery treasures—

to be unburied by your partner.

-
-
- *Key #4: Change It Up*
- When considering change, it's necessary to broaden your experiences. About all the sexual changes some people experience is the "I'll be on top this time" sort. This key will show you how to create such change that your partner will be anticipating what's to come every time you plan (and planning is an essential element) to have sex.
-
- *Key #5: Connecting On All Sexual Cylinders*
- This Key teaches you how to be all-in. You'll discover the incredible heat from a fire that's been fueled by employing all the Keys. Once you have a menu of choices and throw in the emotions felt from a bonded partner, you'll feel

explosively energetic releases.

- We've made some pretty ambitious promises, but let me share with you the reasoning behind this knowledge. There are some biological reasons why these Keys build more passionate lovemaking. No matter what your issues are, learning and practicing these Keys will give you much hotter sexual experiences. However, before you try all these things, you need to rule out a medical condition that could be an underlying, or even primary, issue.
-
- **Medical Reasons for a Decrease in Sexual Desire**
- You would think we'd be over the shame and stigma attached to a decline in sexual drives or having issues with sexual dysfunction. Unfortunately, this is not the case, especially for men. Men identify with their ability to perform,

considering themselves to be less of a man if they aren't able to maintain an erection, or if they have little desire for sex. Although the feelings are different for women, they are no less damaging to their chances of having hot sex. Many women freely talk to other women about feeling sexually obligated or about giving their partner's sex to get something they want in exchange. It becomes a standing joke in female circles that so-and-so must be great in bed to have earned that new car or exciting trip. Exchanging sex for treats reduces passionate sex to how you would reward a dog for being obedient.

- Before we begin discussing the medical and psychological issues that can put out the flame, let's agree to remove the shame or stigma from any problem you might be having. After all, if you had diabetes or high blood pressure, you wouldn't be ashamed, would you? Once the inferior feelings are forgotten, you can get started on overcoming any medical issues that could be the root cause of your inability to have or enjoy great sex.

-

- Two of the most common medical problems that negatively affect your sex life are diabetes and high blood pressure. Females also have a whole other set of issues with the onset of menopause when their hormones tank and the walls of their vagina become thinner and more easily irritated. Younger women can also have hormonal issues when they are breastfeeding. This, however, is not a complicated fix. Most of the time, with a slight change in hormones, they are back to hot sex.

-

- People who have thyroid problems or issues with

chronic depression are also susceptible to lower sex drives. If you have nerve damage brought on by Parkinson's, multiple sclerosis, or have had pelvic surgery, these things can impact your ability to enjoy or want sex (4).

- All these issues can be improved or eliminated by consulting with and following the advice of a professional. Let's examine some things you can do to improve your sex drive.

-

-

-

- **Things You Can Do to Improve Your Sex Drive**

1. Get plenty of sleep.
2. A study done by the University of Chicago revealed that people who sleep less than five hours a night for an extended period will experience the testosterone levels of someone 15

years older (2).

3.

4. Reduce stress.

5. Stress hormones like cortisol and adrenalin cause resistance to testosterone. Dr. Malcolm Carruthers, founder of the Centre for Men's Health, says: *"I do believe testosterone deficiency is becoming more common and happening younger. It used to affect mostly men in their 50s, but it's now men in their 40s and even their 30s (2)."*

6. Reduce or eliminate the use of alcohol and drugs.
7. It also helps to lay off the cigarettes.
8.

9. Eat well and maintain a healthy weight.
10. Carrying additional belly fat can block testosterone.
11.

12. If sex is painful for you, don't always make it about intercourse. Spend more time enjoying the foreplay. Also, try different positions. You may

find some more comfortable and less painful than others. It's always a good idea to empty your bladder before sex as well (5).

13.

14. It's easy to know when to contact a professional. The answer is—right away. Don't wait for years to pass without enjoying great sex. Avoid letting physical issues create emotional stress on you and your partner.

15. When you've cleared up any medical reasons that may be prohibiting your ability to reignite the fire in your relationship, then it's time to move on to the five most important Keys that can help you put the heat back into your sex life.

16.

17.
18.
19.
20.
21.
22.
23. CHAPTER 2
24.
25. Secret key #1
26.
27.
28.
29. Making a game-time decision
30.
31.
32.
33. Obviously, you have a decision to make. This Key can be the most difficult one used to unlock the secrets to lighting that fire in your relationship. The longer you have let your sex life cool, the more difficult it will be to heat

things up. Although the decision will be yours to make, you will need open communications and full cooperation with your partner as well. It's a two-fold issue: (1) making the decision; and (2) getting your partner on board with your plan.

34. You'll notice I have referred to this process as a "game-time" decision. Let me explain what I mean by that term. A game-time decision is usually one made just at the time of play—at the exact time things need to happen. All the preparation has gone into making the decision, and then it is time to jump in and start the game. That's what it's going to be like to begin using the Keys for improving your sex life. All the preparation in the world isn't going to make that moment you decide to jump in any less awkward or stressful. What it will do is give you the courage and confidence that you are doing the right thing.

35. So, let's examine all the elements of preparation that will lead up to your game-time decision. You'll need to take into consideration the following points before communicating your plan to your partner.

36.

37.

38.

39. Prepare for that Game-time Move

40. Deciding to embrace the Keys to hot sex is no easy endeavor. It's important to consider the elements that make up good decision-making strategies. The success of this plan could mean a rescued relationship. Don't be fooled into believing that hot sex is always spontaneous. That's the Hollywood version, where people are ripping their clothes off as they come through the door. Not that you won't want to try that strategy later on, but let's get you through the awkwardness first. That way you'll be ready to step up your game as you have some success under your belt—literally.

41. Taking the time to plan your decision to have great sex with your partner won't take the fun out of it, it will turn up the heat. When you've both planned to make your sex exciting, your anticipation will be a huge payoff. So, these are the elements to consider before making your game-time decision.

42. *Uncertainty*

43. Expect, at first, to feel hesitant and uncertain, insecure and uncomfortable. That's what this is all about, to get you out of your comfort zone. If you don't feel these emotions, you haven't created enough change to bring on the heat, to build the fire. Every time couples try new things, every time you get closer to the fire, there's a chance you'll get burned. That's part of the

excitement—taking that chance. So, welcome the insecurity and discomfort; it means you are well on your way to having better sex than you've ever experienced.

44.

45. *Complexity*

46. Many factors will come into play during your decision to reignite the fire in your relationship. Often, the factors that you have to consider will play against one another. For example, you will need to set aside time to build the fire. To do that, it may mean a significant change in your personal schedule, or time taken from other activities to devote to sex. Make your decisions with a clear understanding of how one issue will affect others, then prioritize. What is most important? What will have the greatest impact on your relationship? Somedays hot sex is going to take priority. Somedays, maybe not.

However, if sex never comes first, if you consider sex as something to do to appease your partner when there's nothing better going on, it will eventually make you not want to play.

47.

48. *Consequences*

49. There are going to be consequences to the decisions you make; every decision has its consequences—some good, some bad. What you need to do is be prepared for those consequences. For example, if you decide to role-play, or incorporate adult toys into your new sexual explorations, your partner may not agree or understand your need. Just beginning to have more sex may be a bit of a shock. So, understand that with each decision to step up your game, there will be some consequences. If you decide to build some fear of discovery into your sex life, the consequence might be that you could get

caught. If that consequence isn't real, the fear won't be there.

50. The more creative you become when you use these Keys, the greater your results will be as well. Your response to these consequences will depend on your perception. How do you view the word consequence? A consequence is not good or bad in itself. It's simply what happens as a result of the decisions you make. All you want to do is be able to reasonably predict the consequences of your decisions. This ability to predict leads us to the next element of decision-making.

51. *Reasonably Predict the Outcome*

52. If you have properly considered all your options and consequences, you should have a reasonable idea of the results of your decision. When it comes time to jump in—to make that game-time decision, you'll be prepared for what could

happen. Not to say the unexpected doesn't sometimes throw you a curve ball, but being able to reasonably predict the outcome of your decision will give you the confidence to handle the unexpected.

53. Being on your game means that you will, at times, have to make more game-time decisions. That's okay, this very first decision to jump in will prepare you for other decisions to come.

54.

55. *Plan Your Approach*

56. Postponing your decision to just "do it" until the perfect time, is the coward's way out, and it's no way to reignite the heat. There is no perfect time. It's a game-time decision; the time is right now. However, how you plan to approach your partner needs some preparation. The reason you need a strategy is that all these things will come into play when communicating your needs with

your partner and getting him or her to become a player as well. Building a fiery relationship is a dual effort. You cannot create the heat all by yourself. So, let's discuss how you will approach your partner.

57.

58. *Set the Scene*

59. Discussing your sexual desires with your partner can be quite intimidating, so set the scene. Timing is everything. Don't wait until you're in a heated argument about your partner's inattentiveness or time spent with other people or things to bring up needing to build more fire in your relationship. Doing this will start the process off with a raging, out-of-control fire, and not usually one that lends itself to having great sex. Anger and resentment often act as fire extinguishers. Since you are the one taking the initiative to build this fire, you need to make sure

the winds of discontent aren't blowing so hard that it threatens to either put your fire out or level the city. Setting the scene puts you in control.

60.

61. When you're setting the stage to discuss your sexual needs, create a time and place where your voice will be heard. Make it a time when you have can freely talk about what you want to do for your partner, explaining in sexy detail how you plan to make your partner feel. Remind your lover how things used to be, how hot your sex was when you first met. In fact, bringing up a particularly exciting sexual exchange is an excellent way to get your partner's attention. See what I mean? If properly planned, the conversation alone can be a turn on.

62.

63. *Explore Together*

64. Once you have made yourself vulnerable by sharing what it is you want, get your partner to join in the game. Ask them about their wants and needs. Exploration means sharing the fantasies as well as the practical ideas. During this time of exploration, make it a "no-holds-barred" kind of thing. Anything goes! Keep in mind, you've been planning this for a while, but your partner hasn't. He or she may also be struggling with insecure, uncertain feelings that might surface during your exploration of the possibilities of bringing back the fire. Again, use all your emotions to stimulate and excite one another.

65.

66. It's strange how our minds and bodies react to the unknown. Most of us fear the unknown. Let me share something with you about fear. The physiological feelings one experiences with fear are the same as one experiences when you exchange a spark of interest with a stranger. When your central nervous system has been awakened, your sexual arousal will follow suit (6). The feelings of fear and arousal within your body are the same. The body doesn't know the difference; so, creating a bit of fear can be used to stimulate you and your partner's physical responses during the conversation you are having.

67.

68. Now add touch to the equation, and what you have is the beginnings of a fire, my friend. As you are having this conversation, make sure you are sitting close, touching your partner. At first, the touch can be reassuring, and then see where things go from there.

69. *Create A Vision*

70. Decide ahead of time what you want to happen after having this conversation. If you want it to

lead to hot sex, make it happen. Jump in! It could be a game-time decision that will depend on all the factors and options you have already considered. The beauty of being a visionary is that having that picture and being able to predict the outcome.

71. I'm sure you've heard of athletes who imagine their successful throw of a football or see themselves making a perfect trajectory of the basketball to the hoop. That's what I'm talking about. Create a picture in your mind where you want this conversation to go, and then do what it takes to turn that picture into reality. If you want it to lead to hot sex, create the possibility. If you've communicated the fact that you want to use some sex toys or that you would welcome incorporating some hot videos into your sexual activities, then have those things ready and available.

72.

73. As you are having the conversation with your partner, explaining some of the things you'd like to do, let them know you have those things ready. Perhaps you could even show them what you have in mind as you're talking. All the while you are having this conversation, keep touching and talking. It's like an adult show and tell, don't you think? It won't be a secret to how your partner is responding to your conversation. You'll hear and see the fire grow until the conversation leads to the act.

74.

75. Be open to where the conversation takes you. If you have set the scene for building a great fire, explored your options with your partner, and helped them to feel the heat by creating a vision through the senses, then enjoy the sex. The worst thing to do is cry or become angry if your

partner doesn't respond the way you thought her or she would. Have a screaming match and storming out will make it that much harder to achieve your goal of reigniting the fire in your relationship. You've set yourself up for failure if you sit in your usual TV spots during a football game, agree to turn the sound down but leave the picture on, and clinically talk about your lackluster sex. It's almost a sure thing that after that kind of conversation, you'll have nothing to look forward to but the outcome of the game. If this is how you set the scene, then you've just tried to build your fire in the middle of a torrential downpour. It ain't gonna happen!

76. Some people decide to use the vision approach first. They set the scene and plan on further exploration by creating an atmosphere of surprise. The story of Tasha and Derrick will illustrate what I mean.

77. Tasha and Derrick had been dating for five years, and they had both slipped into the comfort and ease of Saturday "honey dos" and Sunday afternoon sports. Their routine was comfortable and pleasant, but they lacked heat in the romantic department. It's not that they didn't have sex, but it always seemed to follow that same easy, comfortable path as the rest of the time they spent together.

78.

79. Sometimes Derrick and Tasha would decide to watch the football game at the neighbors. If it was a late game, Tasha would sneak out a little early, light up the grill, and have a few burgers or hot dogs ready for dinner when Derrick returned home. This Sunday she decided things were going to be a bit different. Tasha was going to light a fire, but it wasn't going to be for hamburgers. Tasha had made a decision to

create some heat in her and Derrick's relationship, and she had planned well ahead of time.

80.

81. Instead of hamburgers and hotdogs, Derrick came home to a darkened room with burning candles, some large, vibrating toys and an erotic video laying on the coffee table. Next, he saw Tasha standing before him dressed in hot pink lingerie. The communications were clear; there was no need for conversation. Not only had Tasha planned and set the scene, but she already had a good idea of how her partner would react.

82.

83. The evening was a great success, and it led to some intimate conversation afterward. Sometimes the sex comes before the talk. It all depends on your plan. The Key is to make the decision to create the heat, and then make a plan

that serves that purpose. If the unexpected happens, don't let that stop you from dropping back and huddling together to decide where to go from there. A different outcome than you planned doesn't have to be a game-stopper. Try a different approach; that's all.

84.

85.

86.

87.

88.

89.

90. CHAPTER 3

91.

92. SECRET KEY #2

93.

94.

95.

96. KNOW AND SHARE YOUR TURN-ONS

97.
98.
99.

100. You can't share what you don't know. Before you can clearly communicate what makes you hot, you have to take a little self-inventory of your turn-ons. To give you some direction during your discovery process, we have listed some of the

most common things that men and women say turns them on. Let's begin with ten things most men say are their hot buttons:

101.

102. **Ten Things Women Do That Make Men Hot**

1. Men found it sexy when women take the initiative. If you're always the one to want sex, it can make you feel needy and undesirable. Knowing that your lady is looking at you with lust in her eyes is quite erotic. Everybody likes to feel wanted, and nothing sends that message better than a, well let's just put it bluntly, horny woman. If the decision to have sex is always initiated and led by the man, it's often difficult for the male to know if it is something his partner wanted to do or if she's just complying to get it over with so she can watch her favorite television program.

2.

3. The one who initiates sex also has a greater responsibility to make sure it's good. After all, you say to yourself; my partner is the one who wanted to do this—now, it's up to them to make me feel good. Having your partner hot for you takes the weight off your shoulders and lets you sit back and forget about all your cares and responsibilities. It sets your mind free and allows you to focus on all the pleasure your partner is giving you. Not that it is like this all the time, and that's the beauty. But, wow! Who wouldn't like to have those roles changed every once in a while?

4.

5. Men loved their women to wear sexy lingerie or dress the part of the seductress. One gentleman said his partner would do her housework around him in nothing but a thong and stilettos. When I asked him if she ever got tired of walking around

the house cleaning in high heels, he laughed. He eventually hired a housekeeper because her cleaning efforts never got any further than a few pushes with the vacuum and a deep bend in front of him with a dust cloth.

6.

7. Sexy lingerie or skimpy underwear is nothing new as a turn on for men. Some like lingerie so see-through that it's only a hint of covering over the most important parts. Some men like for their partners to leave a little more to the imagination. Or, they like a tightly laced corset with thigh-high nylons. To make it a sure thing, you may want to look through some lingerie photos online or in a magazine together to see what fuels the fire.

8.

9. Foreplay is just plain fun. Women are not alone in their love to practice tantalizing foreplay.

When someone else controls the foreplay, the heat can build to such a crescendo that it threatens your ability to hang on and wait for your partner to reach your ready level. Foreplay can be a number of things, and it doesn't always have to end in intercourse. Some men find it blissfully torturous to have a woman that is proficient in blue-balling. The rise and fall of arousal can build the heat to such intensity that intercourse is almost anticlimactic.

10.
11. Then there are the rather adventurous men who said they loved to watch their woman masturbate and climax as they were instructed on what to do to themselves. They liked seeing the confidence of a woman who wasn't afraid of her sexuality and who didn't act ashamed of her body. Many men also enjoyed the power they have over their partner when they bring her to orgasm.

12.

13. Some men liked to hear the sound of excitement from their partners. They got turned on as their partner's breathing became labored, and then when moans escaped, their need heated up several degrees. Some liked to hear their names spoken or called out. Some wanted it loud and demanding. Others enjoyed just a hint of heat; a soft, horse released breath did the trick. Talking dirty is also an option, but for some partners that can be a definite turn-off. Make sure you define your turn-ons before putting them into play.

14.

15. Some men enjoyed it when their partners squeezed their buttocks or their biceps in the heat of the moment, lifting themselves to the motion of their bodies. Without exception, men said they liked their partners to actively participate, to do a little grind during the

foreplay. Some even wanted their partners to guide their hands to their "hot" spots.

16.

17. Some got turned on by a woman's sense of humor, feeling secure in the knowledge that if he made a mistake, it wasn't going to be earth shattering. It was a turn-on to know that he could let go of the stress and worry to focus on the fun. Isn't that what sex should be—playful and fun?

18.

19. Many men liked their partners to be creative, unafraid to have fantasy sex, willing to have sex on the beach or in their friend's home as they visited for dinner. Anything that added that extra little bit of danger and excitement was enough to turn those embers into a fire.

20.

21. Hands down, every man loves head. There is

something empowering to men to see their partner go down on them and take their manhood in their mouth. One thing to agree upon before giving head is what you want to have happen at the point of climax. That way your man won't be distracted by wondering if he should pull out or not. Giving head is an excellent way to bring your partner to peak level, and then making them wait a bit and settling down until you build the next wave of pleasure. Get up for a minute, walk around nude, stand in front of the bed and let them see your body's responses to his excitement. Then, start all over again. I'm getting hot just talking about it.

22.

23. Most men wanted their partners to be up for anything, open to trying different ways to create hot sex. They wanted their partners to trust them enough to consider extreme fantasies and

creative ways to light them up (7).

24.

25. Okay, now that you know some of the things that men said turned them on, let's discuss what turns on women. Keep in mind; women are more complex creatures when it comes to their sexuality. A woman's turn-ons are often connected to emotional responses as well as their physical needs.

26.

27. Ten Things Men Do That Make Women Hot

1. Women often preferred the lighter touches along their arms, down their backs, on their inner thighs, and brushed against their lips. What can be a turn-off is men who smash into their lips, open their mouths so wide they could swallow a watermelon, and cram their tongues down their throats until they are ready to choke. Even if you're having rougher sex, it never hurts to pull back and lightly appreciate her skin and lips.

2.

3. Most women loved to have their partners run their fingers through their hair. Of course, not when she's all ready to go out, but sitting on the couch during a make-out session or foreplay, scoop her hair back and even hold it a little tighter at the nape of her neck. It's a promise of gentle yet powerful sex. Very hot, guys!

4.

5. Not only did women love the fresh smell of their partners, but they also enjoyed the act of showering together. It can be quite hot to feel each other's slick, soapy skin. A creative combination might be to wash your partner's hair for her while you're showering together. Now you're thinking! Spooning with your partner in the shower lets them feel the full pressure of your excitement as you run your fingers over her

breasts, stomach, and down to her most private places.

6.

7. Women found intelligence a turn-on. They liked their men to know about different things and be willing to talk about what they know. They wanted a man smart enough to challenge them and press them to be better. The mind is probably one of the most neglected sexual parts of one's body. When your partner can capture your thoughts, you can get lost in the process.

8.

9. Women also enjoyed being surprised. Not just presents, either, although they're certainly welcomed once in a while. Surprises come in many different packages. Sometimes a surprise could be fixing the leaking sink that you promised to do two months ago, or making arrangements to have a meal catered in one night. If you want to make it a sexual surprise, linking it with food is always fun. The old whip-cream standby is good, then add a few strawberries and a few ice cubes from your drink, viola—you've got a hot surprise.

10.

11. Women also loved partners who were patient with them. Don't get angry if they got home from work a little late. Avoid losing your temper with them when they take longer than you would like when it comes to putting on their makeup. Regarding foreplay, patience is a total turn-on. Wait for your partner's legs to shake and for her begging to begin before penetration. Believe me; that will sometimes take the patience of a saint— but the heat a patient partner creates is worth the wait.

12.

13. Seductive texting was also a turn-on for women, especially when they'd had a particularly trying day. Instead of asking them what happened, tell your partner you have a way to take her mind off her problems and you plan on showing her when she gets home. Then, make the evening be about her. Give her a massage, from her shoulders, down her back, around to her inner thigh, and to her feet. Use a lubricant, and warm it up to warm her up.

14.

15. Understanding a woman's personal needs will let her know that you know her inside and out. If she is grumpy, don't always think it's something you did, just give her some space. Don't worry the situation or take the blame for something with which you are probably not involved. Don't get pouty and quiet; your partner deserves the chance to express her feelings even if she's grumpy or in a mood. Let her have those feelings, and welcome her back with open arms when she's ready to confide in you. If she doesn't feel like talking, call it good, and cuddle. With her distractions, this may not be a very good time for hot sex, but soft touches and cuddling can let her know you're sensitive to her needs.

16.

17. Women like a well-dressed, freshly scented partner. Be careful about using cologne that's too heavy; you don't want to cover up the delicious smell of hot sex. Have you ever noticed that? Sex has such a warm glowing fragrance to it; you may just want to use soap as a scent and then let your manliness come through. Whenever you go out, your partner is wearing you like a designer accessory. So, make her proud!

18.

19. Most women wanted to hear about their partner's feelings and beliefs. They wanted to know they were special enough for their man to share with them their deepest thoughts and secrets. Talking in bed after sex is an excellent time to do this. It increases the intimacy. Who knows, you could be headed for another fire (8).

20.

21. You may not know yourself well enough or have enough confidence to voice your turn-ons to your partner. That's cool! The process of discovery will be eye-opening. You'll discover, and it will become quite obvious to your partner, the things that send you to the moon and back. If you can't tell your partner with words what you want, show him or her with sexy sounds and let your body speak for you at first. When you see how the Keys turn on the heat, you'll soon find the words to share with your partner all the things you want to have done to you and what you plan to do in return.

22.

23. Try some of these Key things on yourself and with your partner to kick up the heat. Anticipate the amazing sex you'll have together, and share your imaginations and fantasies with your partner. Tell him or her what you plan on doing, and as you're exchanging likes and dislikes, a little bit of showing will go a long way to fan the sexual flames. All I've got to say is—enjoy the fire!

24.
25.
26.
27.
28.
29.
30.
31.
32.
33.
34.

35.
36.
37.
38.
39.
40.
41.
42. CHAPTER 4
43.
44. SECRET KEY #3
45.
46.
47.
48. MAINTAIN THE MYSTERY
49.
50.
51. Insert chapter five text here. Insert chapter five text here. Insert chapter Practicing this Key can be challenging, so let me explain what I mean by maintaining the mystery in your relationship. Can you remember how you

felt about your partner when you began your relationship? You were both eager to learn about one another. It seemed like you just couldn't get enough. You weren't just hungry for their body, but you wanted to have it all—to consume and fold them into you until you knew one another's thoughts before they were spoken words.

52. Wanting to know everything about your partner isn't really what you desired, though. What most people seek is the "want." You want to still "want" to know more about your partner. Does that make sense? When you quit wanting more, you quit altogether. It's the desire that drives the relationship—that creates the intimacy that reignites the fire of your relationship.

53.

54. Mysterious doesn't mean manipulative. Don't play games to purposefully make your partner doubt your relationship or your devotion. That's unfair and cruel, and it will end up backfiring on you in the long run. Being a bit mysterious just means holding back a little for later, saving part of yourself so that your partner enjoys the discovery process. When he or she asks you something, instead of answering, let them know that you'll tell them later. Or, talk to them about how to find the answer to that one for themselves.

55.

56. Be genuine and honest with your partner when you are creating or maintaining the mystery in your relationship. Those of you who have been in a relationship for a long time are probably thinking—it's a bit late for this Key, right? Wrong! For you, instead of holding information back and being mysterious, you have to create new mystic—but how? That's Key #3.

57.

58. **Give Cause to Question**

59. When I say cause to question, I don't mean for you to give your partner cause to question your devotion or loyalty. Give him or her cause to wonder what you have up your sleeve—what is coming next. Be unpredictable. Do the unexpected. Keep your partner guessing, and make it fun and playful. For example, Clair curled up with a good book one cold winter evening. The fire was going, but there was a chill in the air, so she had her flannels on and a cozy cover-up as she laid beside her sweetie on the sofa. You wouldn't exactly call her pajamas sexy, but what she did with them started to light Patrick up.

60.

61. She pulled the covers up to right below her neck as she read her book. At first, Patrick didn't look to see what she was reading. In fact, he paid

little attention to Clair at all. He was busy streaming Facebook and checking his emails. So, she laid her book, print down, on the table so Patrick could see that it was an erotic book. Still acting like nothing was up as she adjusted the covers; then she picked the book back up and continued to read. Only, now that he saw the cover of the book, she had captured his interest. Next, Clair pulled off the bottoms to her pajamas and began playing beneath the covers, while still holding the book. The action beneath the blanket started getting more heated, and Patrick wanted in on the action. It was a fun evening, and it wasn't long before neither Clair nor Patrick needed the covers or the fire; they were making a fire together that made the one in the fireplace unnecessary. Clair never turned a page of that book, and Patrick never noticed because he was busy under the covers with Clair.

62.

63. The reason I share this story with you is that Clair did the unpredictable, and it ended in great sex. She didn't sit down to have a big talk with Patrick; she just started building the fire all by herself and Patrick joined in. What she did was peak Patrick's curiosity, and then teased him into being attentive. There was no nagging or anger, just playful fun. Not only did Clair capture Patrick's attention, but because she has continued now and then to do the unpredictable, Patrick looks forward to what's coming next— besides him.

64.

65. Another element of Clair's sofa surprise is that she kept herself hidden. What is hidden is often more enticing than what is offered in plain sight. If someone walks along a nude beach sporting a skimpy bathing suit while all the other beach people are stark naked, who do you thing gets the most attention? You guessed it, the one that left a little to the imagination.

66.

67.   Don't Always Be Readily Available

68.   It may sound like you're game-playing, and perhaps in a way you are. However, it's a healthy game designed to keep the fire burning in your relationship. What I mean by not always being readily available is this. Don't wait by the phone, picking it up on the first ring, out of breath as if you ran to answer. Don't ask when your partner is going to call, just expect that he or she will. If they tell you they'll give you a call, let them know that you have plans and may not be home so they can leave a message and you'll call them back later. Now you've got them wondering where you are going, who you'll be with, and when you'll call them back. You've created some mystery.

69.

70. Being needy with your partner is like pouring water on the fire. Rarely do others enjoy having to reassure someone all the time by reporting their whereabouts. Don't become an extension of your partner—get a life! Be active with friends of your own. Avoid making your partner responsible for planning your daily activities. In fact, he or she doesn't need to be included in everything you do.

71.

72. Don't Talk Too Much

73. No matter if your relationship is new or you have years of familiarity with one another, avoid talking non-stop about every little insignificant detail of your day. Don't write on your Facebook about everything you did during the day. Although it's great to share things with your lover, does your partner need to know you just picked up a Starbuck's latte? Sometimes, it's fun to send a text to say—*"Guess where I am?"* Then don't respond when he or she returns the text. As predicted, as soon as your partner gets home, he or she will probably be asking about that text.

74.

75. People who talk too much about themselves can completely shut down their partners with the same old boring chit-chat. Learn to be an attentive listener. Get your mind out of yourself and into your partner. When you talk, share things that matter to your partner—perhaps something new you discovered about his or her favorite activity, sport, or hobby. Let them know you are thinking of them.

76.

77. Some Things Are Better Left to the Imagination

78. This is especially true if you've been together for

quite some time and the fire in your relationship is only showing a few flumes of smoke—if that. What I mean by this is, when you're doing private things, to keep them private. For example, when you use the potty, shut the door. When you are coloring your hair, do it at a time when your partner is out with friends. When the "boys" are itchy, avoid spreading your legs open on the couch in front of the game and giving yourself a three-minute scratch down. Believe me, when I tell you, this is far from a fire builder. Some things are better done in private.

79.

80. Most bathroom grooming should be done alone unless of course, you're using the shower as an enticement. Make the bathroom a place of sexy fun, not a place where your partner is exposed to all your daily duties. If your dog leaves the bathroom when you've entered, it's a clear sign that what routinely goes on in there needs to be private. Enough said!

81.

82.

83.

84. Challenge Your Partner

85. A little healthy competition can raise the heat in a relationship. Competitive activites should be something that you enjoy together. If you have a sport that both of you participate in, make it competitive. If you don't do any activities together, you've got to challenge yourself to find one. It's important that you find activities that can be enjoyed together. It gives you something to talk about and a time of fun together. It also lets you show off your prowess and strength. If the sport is swimming, that could open up a whole new set of skills.

86.

87. Challenging your lover doesn't always have to be in the form of sport. You can test them in a computer game, playing cards, or even just making a bet. Who knows, the payoff can be quite rewarding for both of you.

88.

89.

90.

91. Let Your Partner Earn Your Compliments

92. Avoid fishing for compliments—it's just another way you show your insecurities. Women can be particularly guilty of this. They'll ask if they look too fat in this outfit, or become offended if their partner doesn't compliment their new hairdo or designer shoes. One lady has a unique way of knowing when her rather undemonstrative partner thinks she looks extra special. He has a dead giveaway sign that he's impressed. He raises his eyebrows when he sees her. That's all

—raised eyebrows?

93.

94. Yep, what this woman has learned is to recognize even the smallest signal from her partner. She knows she looks good, and she's never been one to like lavish compliments. Instead, she searches her partner's face for those telltale raised brows to celebrate her exceptional appearance. What's more, she's learned to return the favor. There have been times when they are across the room at a party, and she will give him that look, raise a dainty little brow, touch her finger to her parted lips, and build a long-distance fire that they both know won't be able to be enjoyed for a few hours. The anticipation is deliciously hot.

95.

96. Encourage Silent Communication

97. These kinds of communications are only between the two of you, creating together the mystery that nobody else can share. These types of silent communications should be little tidbits of information to which only you and your partner are privy. For instance, you may want to whisper in your lover's ear as you go into a restaurant that you feel naked without wearing panties, or ask him to see if he thinks anyone could tell that you are not wearing a bra.

98.

99. One gentleman told me of a time he was at his tennis club, and he found himself being turned on by watching his lover compete in the final round. After she had won the match, he gave her their silent signal, and together they celebrated her win in the club's darkened supply room. Everyone had left, or so they hoped, and it was just them, the linens, and that lovely musky smell of hot sex. The point is, they had a shared secret, a wonderfully mysterious way to communicate their needs that left out the rest of the world.

100.

101. Create the Mystery

102. When you have been together for quite some time, it takes a bit more work to create mystery in your relationship. You have already shared so much information and know each other so well, that you can practically finish one another's sentences. So, you may think this Key is not going to be possible for you. Not so! It may be a little more challenging for you to create opportunities to be mysterious, but that element of surprise and the knack of being unpredictable will be your ticket to success.

103. Speaking of tickets, one lady shared this interesting story. She felt her partner needed a little space in their relationship. So, she bought tickets for him and a buddy to go to the football game. When she gave him the tickets, she also informed him that she'd be waiting for him when he returned with another surprise. Then she said, if the lights are out when you get home, don't sit down and snack in front of the television. Come on into the bedroom. I'll be waiting there for you with your surprise.

104. He was so excited thinking about what she had planned that there were times he found it impossible to focus on the game. Although his buddy wanted to stop for a drink after the game, her partner politely refused. He had better things to do.

105.

106. Creating and maintaining the mystery in a relationship builds excitement and anticipation of a hot encounter. It takes planning and effort, but the results are well worth it. This, in fact, is one of the Keys that can be the most fun and playful. The fire that these sexual games put into your relationship is so memorable that just reminding your partner of them at another time will tease the senses.

107. I challenge you to be creative with this Key and make your sex unique and individual. Create private communications and develop an intimate language that is only understood by you and your partner.

108.

109.

110.
111.
112.

113.

114.
115.

116.
117. CHAPTER 5
118.

119. SECRET KEY #4
120.
121.
122.
123. CHANGE IT UP
124.
125.

126. Although we've talked a great deal about different things you can do to build the heat, keep in mind anything you repeatedly do creates a routine. Between the games, the positions, the toys, and techniques, sometimes your partner just wants comfortable, nurturing, gentle love-making for a change. All of the Keys you use are designed to please and stimulate, but changing things up lets you excite your partner and have great sex irrespective of their attitude or mood.

127.

128. To know when to play and when to put playfulness aside and just focus on body worship, you have to be able to read your partner. Being attentive and sensitive to your partner's feelings and emotions are paramount to using these Keys. Your flexibility and desire to please your partner must trump your desire to please yourself. If your partner needs to be nurtured and cuddled, then that should be your focus. If your partner needs to feel empowered, then do what's necessary to fulfill that need.

129.

130. We've offered you a treasure chest of golden Keys to reignite the fire in your relationship, but being willing to change and use these Keys will determine how much heat you can create. To continue to build the fire, refuse to allow yourself to do one thing most of the time. Change things up, be creative, be unpredictable, be fun and playful, be tender, be rough—but most of all be knowledgeable about all the things you can do to keep the fire burning.

131.

132. The idea of changing things up is not just a clever ploy; it's a scientific fact that people need change. Studies have shown that dopamine decreases over time with the same sexual partner. Does this mean you must find another partner? Not necessarily. Let's discuss how our dopamine levels come into play when we're feeling all the pleasures of incredible sex.

133.

134. I don't mean to over-simplify, but I also don't want to reduce dopamine into a scientific discussion about neurons and transmitters, either. Dopamine is commonly called the pleasure chemical. It is that magical molecule that gladly supports all our most sinful habits and cravings, as it passes along pleasure signals to reward us when we have sex or feel lustful. Increases in dopamine keep us coming back for more. Sometimes you don't even have to have sex, just be reminded of it when smelling perfume or cologne associated with an exciting sexual encounter, and your dopamine levels begin to increase (9).

135.

136. Changing it up can cause the sexual excitement that stimulates an increase in dopamine levels, making it possible to have hot sex without the need to change partners every few months. The more creative and imaginative you are when it comes to changing things up, the greater your chances will be to reignite the fire in your current relationship. Emotionally bonding with another partner takes time and energy, so why not build a sensual fire with the person to whom you are already attached?

137.

138. Not only can you change things up by

creating mystery and employing new devices that stimulate your imagination as well as your body, but you can change where and when you have sex as well. Once you have experimented in every room in your home, take it outside. Expand your sex to include public places where the chances of you getting caught increase your excitement. Talk about sex and get your partner aroused at a time when there is no possible way to satisfy your need for hours, and then watch the fire build. Tory and Malcolm know the value of applying this Key to their sex life.

139.

140. Malcolm teased Tory late one afternoon before going to their in-laws for dinner. They showered together, getting one another quite lathered up, and then Malcolm remembered something he had to do before leaving. In a rush, with many apologies, he hoped out of the shower, leaving Tory in a state of unsatisfied heat. All the way to his in-laws, Malcolm kept saying that he was sorry and promised to make it up to her later. This only served as a reminder of what she had missed.

141.

142. The whole evening, Malcolm would glance at Tory, with a promise of pleasure when they got home, and all the while Tory and Malcolm's dopamine levels were skyrocketing. Every once in a while, Malcolm would slide his hand up Tory's leg beneath the table to keep her body engaged as well as her mind. Dinner ended early that evening, and they rushed back home for a desert of a different kind.

143.

144. Changing it up almost always involves some additional tools of the trade, you just need to be sure you are both in agreement with whatever activities sound interesting. If you lack imagination and creativity, watch the movie *"Fifty Shades of Grey,"* and pick up some helpful information. Not that you'll want to go to that extreme, but experimenting is allowed. While you're at it, watch the movie with your partner. It will give you a chance to build and fire and discuss your sexual likes and limits.

145.

146. Tools and Toys

147. To help you out, we have included some interesting tools and toys to enhance your sex life. The beauty of these devices is that you can shop for them discreetly online. If you have done so, you'll be quite entertained by their variety and scope. You'll find toys that vibrate, gyrate, and pulsate. You'll find devices in all colors and textures, with ones designed to fit inside, outside, and even on your fingers. For those of you who plan on water sports, you'll be happy to know that many are toys are waterproof. If your changeup includes postponing sex and building the fire, you'll find devices that can be worn in the underwear or tucked securely inside the body that can be controlled remotely. These types of toys can create a whole other kind of mystery and secret signal, right?

148.

149. Sexually stimulating toys are not just to pleasure women, but many are specially designed just for men. What used to be intimidating for men is now not only acceptable but eagerly anticipated. An online survey was done in 2014 of 5,000 men. The study was conducted to discover how men felt about the use of sex toys. They found that 51 percent of men owned sex toys, 60 percent said they had used them on their partners, and it was extremely enjoyable.

150.

151. Included in these toys for men are vibrating cock rings, to contain the heated variety if that peaks your interest. There are butt plugs, and sleeve or pocket vaginas that can be filled with a wide range of excitable ingredients. If anything, just shopping for the toys can be an awesome experience for you and your partner. Shop together and double your fun. It's a great way to introduce the new possibilities, to bring up the fact that you want to increase the heat in your sex life. Just tell your partner you want to do some online shopping together for some special surprises.

152.

153. For you who enjoy living on the edge, there are the extreme toys. These are used in couples' bondage games which combine pleasure with a little sting. They include floggers, blindfolds, ropes, handcuffs, and chains. These types of toys are usually for the more seasoned sexual appetites, but having a knowledge of such activities is a good thing just in case you decide to take a giant step outside your comfort zone.

154.

155. It's a good thing most people are past the idea that sex toys are weird, and boy are we past it! Adult toys in North America alone is a $500,000 a year industry, worldwide it has exploded to a multi-billion-dollar business (10). The choices are endless, and they also include lubricants, which can be purchased as all natural, organic, and water soluble products. There are lubricants that provide various sensations, like tingling, warmth, and icy cool, so you can experiment and determine which ones tickle your fancy. They come in almost any flavor under the sun or have no taste at all. Some are smooth textured, and some are granulated. So many choices—so little time.

156.

157. Pricing for your sex toys is about as varied as the products, beginning as low as $5 on up to $200 plus. My point is, and I hope this important Key has demonstrated that there are so many things you can incorporate into your sex life to reignite the fire in your relationship. Some techniques or toys you may not like, but you won't know how to change it up without doing some investigating. You will know your partner's likes and dislikes better if you explore your options together, and now you can do so in the privacy of your home.

CHAPTER 6

SECRET KEY #5

CONNECTING ON ALL SEXUAL CYLINDERS

Connecting with your partner on all levels takes your experience a whole level up. No-emotion sex is good, but when you connect physically and emotionally, it's unbelievable. The more you can connect with your partner, the more you'll want to. All the games, toys, movies, lingerie, or erotica cannot give you that "as one" connection if it doesn't come with deep emotional commitment to your partner. That's what is called connecting on all sexual cylinders.

175.

176. When the heat is high and so is your emotional connection, sex becomes love-making. When your fire is burning strong, and you're implementing all the Keys you've learned, your love-making can reach euphoric heights. It takes all the Keys. You have to make a conscious decision to build the heat into your relationship. Then, discover and share your turn-ons with your partner. Be unpredictable, do the unexpected to maintain some mystery in your relationship. Get creative and be willing to change it up so that the fire doesn't die. Lastly, apply all the Keys to keep the fire going, each partner eager to experience the next sexual encounter.

177. This is your opportunity to transform yourself into a sexual beast. At work you may be the best nurse or lawyer, but once you get home, you can change into a pornstar. Okay, it doesn't have to be that extreme, but you will discover some additional perks when you can heat up your relationship. Great sex can change other aspects of your life as well.

178.

179.

180. Hot Sex Can Change Your Professional Prowess

181. When you are more confident with your sexual self, it changes your level of confidence and your ability to communicate. Let's face it, the more confident you become, the more likely you are to be valued at work. When you are perceived as a valued worker, the monetary rewards soon follow. Also, your ability to communicate is greatly enhanced with a "hotter" sex life. Why? To have a great sex life, you have to be an excellent communicator—with your body language as well as your words.

182.

183. Today's workers, whether white or blue collar, deal with a tremendous amount of stress. If that pressure is allowed to build, it can turn you into a discontent complainer. Your energy level goes down, and you find yourself depressed and unhealthy. Before you realize it, you're taking more sick days or personal time, and still you feel tired. Those who allow themselves to be lackluster sexual partner soon become unenthusiastic business partners.

184.

185. Hot sex also makes the participants able to concentrate and focus more at work. Once you've learned the Five Keys to reigniting your relationship, you have to get creative and be determined to put them into practice. Your focus and concentrated effort brings you great rewards, and so your brain begins to conceive of other ways to focus and concentrate. It's only natural that you take these skills to the workplace.

186. Also, practicing the Five Keys taps into your creative side. Even those that haven't previously considered themselves to be imaginative will be much improved after implementing the Five Keys into their relationships. That same creative effort will also spread into your career efforts, giving you the willingness to try different problem-solving strategies or office management techniques. By building the fire in your relationship, you can also create greater opportunities for success in other areas of your life.

187.

188.

189.

190. **Hot Sex Makes You More Attractive**

191. Have you ever heard people say, *"Oh, you must have got some last night?"* Even if you didn't, why would people say that? It's because most people recognize the difference in one's appearance when they have recently had hot sex. Their skin glows. They walk taller. Their smile is wider. They're more patient. They're more accepting of new ideas. It's a commonly accepted fact that people who regularly have great sex are just more fun to be around. More people are attracted to individuals who ooze sexual energy, and you can't help but do so when you're still experiencing the aftermath of an intense sexual encounter.

192.

193. I've heard it said that sexier people are more active and that increased activity helps you to be less stressed and more youthful. When you are enjoying a raging fire in your relationship, you'll want to look and feel your best outside the bedroom. Your body image will improve, and you will have a little spring in your step (11).

194.

195.

196. You'll Identify with Your Newly Discovered Sexuality

197. Many people who have accepted a life of boring sex or no sex at all, have learned to compartmentalize their lives. They often will share with their closest confidant that their relationship is great—all but the sex, that is. What they have done is create a separate box in which to store their unsatisfactory sex. Once tucked away, it doesn't have to cause them discomfort or embarrassment anymore. These people have become masters at disassociating their sex lives from all the other elements that make them unique.

198.

199. Just as those having great sex become better all-around individuals, people who suffer the pangs of separating their souls from their sex lives begin to see the negative impact that separation can cause in their lives. Our sexual prowess has a direct correlation with our self-perception and how others see us as well. Like it or not, we are often defined by our sexuality.

200. If you want to experience life to its fullest, you have to do it all—including sex. It isn't all about sex, but sex is an important part of all our lives. If sex is so important to our well-being, then why settle for just "so-so" sex? Why not crank up the heat, ignite the flame of desire you once had and bring sex back to life? Nobody will appreciate it more than your partner—except maybe you.

201.

202. You now have a sexual toolbox, filled with all the elements of the Five Keys. If these Five Keys are to be beneficial, you have an important choice to make. Do you finish the book and do nothing, wishing off and on you had the nerve to apply the Keys to your sex life? Or, do you get started immediately on ways to build a fire in your relationship? It's imperative to know that by saying yes to change, it will require something from you. You now have a responsibility to do the work, to keep the fire burning, to increase the heat, and to share more of yourself with your partner.

203.

204.

205. All strong people have vulnerabilities; all have weaknesses that can either be hidden or used to bring about great changes in their lives. Your sexuality carries with it great power, opportunities, and incredible rewards if you say yes to putting the Five Keys to work for you and your partner. By applying these Keys, you and your partner's lives will be enriched and energized. It won't take long, either. Just a lot of practice, but who's going to complain about having more fiery sex?

206.

207. It's never too late to practice the Five Keys. If you think your relationship is too cold to try, what have you got to lose? If you or your partner is about to walk anyway, you've got nothing to lose, right? If you move on to greener pastures, you can pack up your Keys and take them with you. If you have no partner to practice them with, that's okay. You can practice alone and get to know your turn-ons that much better. If you are to have a start-over, you will know better this time around.

208.

209. However, if there are still some embers burning in this relationship, try rekindling them. Even if you have some other challenges, all relationships have challenges. Guess what? Many of those challenges are caused by boring sex or no sex at all. The decision you make right now can be life altering, no kidding! Don't believe me? Give it a try—see for yourself. All it takes is a decision to apply the Five Keys and bring on the heat, in this relationship or another.

210.

211. Have you decided? Good! Now turn off the television, slip into something more revealing, put down this book, and let it burn, baby.

212.
213.
214.
215.
216.
217.
218.
219.
220.
221.
222.
223.
224.
225. Bonus Section 3
226.
227. Intimate

and Lasting Relationships & Marriage
228.
229.
230. J. S. PARKER

231.
232. CONTENTS
233.
234.

Introduction	137
Chapter 1: Why Is A Passion-Filled Marriage Important?	139
Chapter 2: Secret Key #1 – Communication and Understanding	145
Chapter 3: Secret Key #2 – Being Open-Minded	162
Chapter 4: Secret Key #3 – Making Time For Yourselves	177
Chapter 5: Secret Key #4 – Being Intimate with One Another	188
Chapter 6: Secret Key #5 – Finding A Common Interest	199
Chapter 7: Special Useful Tips	209
Conclusion	213

J.

J.

Introduction

Are you in a marriage that is leaving you lost and confused? Do you feel like the intimacy is fading? Are you just looking for a way to strengthen your bond with your spouse? If you have then you have downloaded the right book. In this book, you will find out more about the five secret keys to an intimate and passion-filled relationship. Find out what these keys are and what are the accompanying secrets that they will unlock in your partner and your marriage. You will be inspired to make these changes once you realize how simple yet how commonly overlooked these aspects are in any relationship. Do not make the mistake that most couples make and start picking up these keys and using them like they were always meant to be used.

This book is catered to those who strive to become more intimate and passionate with their partner. If you knew the secrets to unlocking the potential in your marriage, the level of intimacy will never be the same again. Be one of those special individuals that serve as a catalyst towards a better marriage for you and your spouse even if he or she does not even recognize there is a problem. If you resonate at all with the above, please read on to find out more about how to make that strong marriage happen.

Everyone needs this book. Whether you are married, currently in a relationship, wanting to get in one, gay or straight. You need this book. It is the difference between a mediocre relationship and a phenomenal one.

I'd like to thank you first of all for purchasing this book, and I sincerely hope you enjoy it.

CHAPTER 1

Why An intimate and passion-filled marriage is important?

Any marriage must have passion and intimacy to succeed. You can't have a marriage where you two are complacent with each other. That is when the problems set in with infidelity, boredom, and sometimes, even divorce. Use this book as a tool to keep these problems at bay.

Don't get me wrong every marriage has its problems, but when you are passionate about each other, those problems seem minuscule, and they are a lot easier to get over than if you are bored with each other.

What a Passion-filled Marriage is Like

Imagine a marriage where you are gone all day, and all you can think about is rushing home to be with your spouse, just like in the honeymoon phase of your marriage. Now, imagine that you are still wanting to do that after ten years of marriage. The feeling of butterflies in your stomach at the thought of seeing your lover's face after a long day of work is unmatched by any other feeling in the world.

An intimate relationship is filled with love and compassion for the other person, but it is also interesting. It is never knowing what surprises lie in store, but trusting your partner, knowing they will be good.

Have you read any adult novels? The steamy, hot, romantic ones? Imagine having a marriage like that, twenty years into the future of your marriage. It may be unthinkable now, but after you read this book, and apply these five keys to your life, and your marriage, this will be your life.

Why You Should Strive for This

Marriage isn't easy. It comes with a myriad of challenges and obstacles that you have to overcome. That is a part and parcel of marriage. What's not so good is if your marriage comes to a point that you end up being bored with your partner, this is a red flag that you need to quickly address. You definitely do not want to wait until the point that boredom leads to a black and gray picture. You want to add the colors back before it starts fading and to make it the most beautiful picture ever seen. Able to visualize and recall what a scene of that nature looks like? Fascinating isn't it?

Well what can happen if you do not address the problems and obstacles that arise in your marriage early on? Well on the top of my head, boredom can easily lead to infidelity. Ever felt that you were yearning for someone else to fulfill the needs that you have? Well that's not a good sign right there. That feeling stem from your spouse now shouldn't it?

Infidelity is not the only problem that stems from boredom. Constant bickering is another one that can be detrimental to marriages. Once you get bored with someone, you begin to want something more to interest you, and you may start nitpicking at little things that don't even really bother you. Like the fact that your spouse left a spoon unwashed in the sink. You take that little issue and turn it into a full out fight because you are so tired of the silence. The funny thing is, you probably don't even realize that you are doing it either. You just subconsciously want to ease the constant humdrum feeling of the household.

Along with these, boredom can split your marriage apart. You just don't want to be with someone who is not passionate about you. So you decide to leave. You leave the person you love, and break your own heart, because you can't stay another minute in a lackluster relationship. Divorce is expensive, so maybe you just separate for a while, but it still takes its toll on your family. Especially if you have kids.

An intimacy filled relationship is key for a long successful marriage. If you are intimate and passionate about each other, then you will find a whole new world out there waiting for you to reach out for it. This world is full of fun adventures and happiness.

What to Expect From This Book

In this book you will find the next five chapters are the Keys to a passionate marriage. Each chapter is a different key. You have to read on to find out what those keys are. That is why it is called a secret. Each of the keys will have information to help you understand more how to go about using that key to unlock another section of your marriage. There will be different scenarios for some keys that may involve separate information for couples with kids, couples trying for kids, and couples without kids.

There will also be a chapter towards the end on what to expect once the honeymoon is over for newlyweds. This chapter can be skipped if you already have passed that phase in your marriage.

There will also be a chapter on how to recognize if your relationship is unhealthy, or just on the rocks, and information on how to leave a relationship if it is unhealthy/abusive.

Why You Need These Keys

These keys unlock secret parts of a marriage that only a handful of couples have managed to reach. Without them you can have a normal marriage, and even one filled with love, but to truly be at a level beyond your peers and the average couple, you need to master these keys and locks to truly be in the stratosphere of your relationship. Do note that every relationship is different, and that everyone goes through unique circumstances that cannot be accounted for and addressed for every situation. You will have to adapt the scenarios in this book to fit your life. Ultimately you will have to discover what works and how best to implement it. I will do my best to make it very practical and applicable to most scenarios, giving you examples and case studies to illustrate the points that I am driving home. Okay enough of the jibber jabber. Now here comes the fun part! Read on to find out what each key is, and why you need it to make your marriage just that much more special.

Chapter 2

secret key #1

Communication and Understanding

This is perhaps the most important key in any successful happy and passionate relationship. Without this as a foundation, it is difficult to build on other facts that brings out the best in your relationship with your spouse. I decided to put it first, front and center so that you will remember it better.

Simply put, communication and understanding are keys that most people don't even realize the importance of. This one isn't fully a secret, but the depth of it is. Sixty percent of couples do not realize that communication is about more than what you want to eat, and how you are feeling that day. Communication is telling you partner your favorite color, what your first bike looked like, and if you sucked your thumb as a kid. All the little details you would find odd that anyone would want to know, is everything that your partner should know, and vice-versa.

Understanding goes beyond being okay when someone makes a human mistake. Understanding is having the compassion to anticipate the needs of your spouse, while also realizing they are human and can be irrational. It is wanting to know why they sucked their thumb as a child. It is wanting to know what causes their nightmares. It is wanting to be there for them every step of the way in life. That is understanding.

Without these two elements in their fullest, you cannot truly know your partner. You will not be able to truly live in harmony, because you will not be able to understand why they do some of the things they do, and you will not be able to communicate why you are frustrated. This key unlocks compassion. True compassion for another person. The kind you wish the world would show you.

Communication is a big key in a marriage, because without it, you don't know what the other person is thinking. You aren't a mind reader, and you should not be expected to be. So you have to communicate. You have to speak up about what you are thinking. Whether it be if the other person hurt you, or if you want something. You can't get mad at someone for not doing something they had no idea they were supposed to be doing.

The other side of that discussion is you also have to be understanding when your partner is telling you something. It is really hard for communication to flow freely, when your spouse is afraid to tell you something, because they are afraid that you will get mad.

Understanding your partner also goes deeper than just being understanding. You also have to understand their wants and needs. Eventually you will learn to anticipate those, but for now, you have to focus on what they are trying to say, even if they aren't able to fully express it themselves. This goes for in and out of the bedroom. You have to love your spouse enough to learn everything about them, that way you can understand them better.

You are probably needing a lot more information on these subjects, so they will be broken down with more information, starting with communication.

Communication

Have you ever been mad at your spouse for not being romantic enough, or not taking out the trash or doing the dishes? Chances are you probably have. Think back to the last time you were angry at your spouse for something like that. Did you tell them that you wanted it done? No? Then why are you angry? It's not like they were ignoring you. Your spouse didn't know that he or she was supposed to do these things because you did not specify your desire for them to be done.

Lack of communication leads to unnecessary fighting, and that makes your household miserable, and a miserable household is not one filled with passion. You have to talk to your partner. There are many ways to begin telling them what is bothering you, if you are not sure how to begin.

You can start by writing everything down, and giving it to them. This may seem like a juvenile thing to do, but if you are not great at expressing desire or emotions, it is a helpful tool that will allow you to get everything out without a problem. They also can't interrupt you, because you aren't physically speaking. Writing your feelings down can also help you decide if you are being irrational. It is actually a good idea to write them down, even if you plan on speaking your mind, because you can make yourself sound more rational to save saying something that you will regret.

If you can communicate rationally, then you can sit down, and have a heart-to-heart chat about things that are bothering you. Take turns saying your what's on your mind and take turns listening to your partner's. Sometimes, you feel a lot better getting it off your chest, rather than just bottling it up. Because when you bottle something up, it just builds and builds and builds, until you finally snap. This is the cause of a lot of problems, because you snap at your partner for no apparent reason, due to the fact that you are just now showing anger over something that happened two weeks ago.

However, if you fight over everything, and even written communication doesn't help, then you can try a technique that has helped save many marriages. You schedule an argument where you plan to get everything out on the table that has made you angry recently. Before you start the argument, buy a couple of helium-filled balloons. Roll a die to see who has the floor first. Highest number wins. Once you figure out who has the floor first, that person pokes a hole in their balloon and sucks the helium out. Be sure to pinch the hole closed while you are talking so the helium doesn't escape cause you are going to need to refill your lungs a couple of times.

Once you have filled your lungs with helium, it is time to start talking. Talk about everything that bothers you, big and small, until you start laughing. If you can't be angry about it while speaking in a chipmunk voice, then it wasn't worth getting angry in the first place. Once you both have said your piece, go over what you were angry enough about to say even though your voices were distorted hilariously. Try to find solutions to those problems. Once you can find a solution to your problems, you will be able to avoid having those same problems in the future.

Be Honest

Communication is not just calling out your spouse when they have done something wrong. It is also admitting when you mess up as well. If you make a mistake, tell your partner, and let them know how much you truly regret it.

Being honest is hard, but if you do or say something that you know will hurt your partner to find out about, it is best to tell them yourself. If they hear it from someone else, it is liable to ruin your relationship. However, if they hear it from you directly, they may hurt for a while, but they will respect you for telling the, the truth.

However, honesty is not just about when you do something wrong, it is also about telling your partner the truth whether they want to hear it or not. Say you are a guy, and your wife is putting on her makeup. She finishes, and thinks she looks great, but it makes her look a little clownish. Kindly tell her that it is a bit much. Offer some suggestions to make it look better without her having to redo everything. As angry as she may be, it is better for you to tell her, than for her to hear it from some snickering strangers. If she decides to still go out like that, then it is her choice and you must support her, but you should always warn her first.

Say you are a woman, and your husband wears nothing but Hawaiian shirts and cargo shorts, and you wish he would wear something different once in a while. Be honest with him. Tell him you love him for who he is, but sometimes a change is refreshing. Offer some suggestions that he might like, and if he still refuses, accept it and move on. You cannot change them, but they don't know you don't like something unless you tell them.

Be honest about your plans. Don't tell your spouse that you are going somewhere, and be somewhere else entirely. Even if you think they will get mad about where you plan to go, it is always best to be honest, because if something were to happen to you, and you weren't where you say you were, they would have no idea where to start looking. You have to be open and forthcoming with information always, otherwise, you can break your partner's trust, or worse, you could get hurt and they wouldn't know what happened.

As difficult as it can be to be honest sometimes, it is necessary. You have to be truthful. If you are honest with your partner, it will strengthen their trust in you, and they will love you even more knowing that they can always count on you to do the right thing, no matter how hard it is.

Communication in its entirety can save a marriage, as you are getting things off your chest, and working to fix problems. Finding solutions together will bring you closer together as a couple, and ignite the passion in your marriage. You will find that things get a whole lot more steamy and intimate when you start opening up and being honest with each other.

Understanding Your Partner

Everyone has their quirks. We all have something that makes us different from everyone else. And while that is endearing, because it makes us unique, these quirks can also cause a problem in a marriage where couples don't understand them.

Early on in the marriage, during the honeymoon stage, everything is a wonderful bed of thorn-less roses. You get up, enjoy each other's company and are full of love for each other, but as you discover more and more about your partner, you find there are more and more things that you don't understand. This is normal. You are just learning about your partner, and you are not expected to know everything about them yet.

However, if something they do bothers you, ask them about it. Try to understand why it is that they do what they do. Understand who they are, and always understand that they are only human, they are not perfect.

Understanding Their Needs

Understanding your partner goes beyond understanding the things they do. It also branches out into understanding their needs, and being able to anticipate their wants. This does not come immediately and it takes some work. You have to communicate to get to this phase. Talk about what you like, and your hobbies, and what you want from life. There are basic needs however that you should know about.

These needs differ between the sexes.

Men

Men are seen as tough, indestructible creatures because that is what society imposes on them. They are expected to be the breadwinners of the family, and to never show emotion. This is the farthest thing from the truth. Men need a safe place to show their emotions, and they too need a shoulder to cry on at times.

Men need to feel validated. They need to be told how important they are, and not be taken for granted. Society dictates that a man already know how important he is and that he is an egotistical brute. Society is wrong. Often times men are just as insecure as women. They need to be told how good they look, and be told that they are appreciated.

Men go through a lot. They work hard all day to help pay the bills (in most cases). They come home, and love on their spouses, and if they have them, children. They just want to sit in a chair and eat dinner and then go to sleep. However, doing this can lower a man's self-esteem, as he feels he is letting the household down. Men need an extra chore around the house to feel like they are helping their spouses, even if the spouse doesn't work. Ask him to take out the trash. He will groan about it, but deep down he will enjoy doing something that makes your life a little easier.

In turn, you should make his life a little easier. Don't complain about every little thing. This is where understanding comes in. Rather than complain, voice your concerns kindly, and help try to find solutions to the problems. This makes the household a less stressful environment, and makes it more enjoyable.

Men are seen as creatures that always want sex. This is not always true. However, if he wants sex often and you don't, don't gripe at him on a day where you want sex and he doesn't. If you are allowed to not be in the mood, so is he. It does not mean he is cheating on you. Chances are, if he has a high libido, he just rubbed one out right before you asked, and is embarrassed to tell you. Or maybe he just had a bad day, and just wants to cuddle and talk about it. Be there for him like he is there for you.

There are a lot more needs that men have, but those are more controversial. Just be there for him. Your husband needs to feel loved and secure in your marriage. This is one thing that doesn't change across the board.

Women

Women are very strong beings. While that is very much true, there are times when women also want to have the chance to be vulnerable and to depend on their man. With that said, it is statistically proven that women don't want their men to be to clingy. So bottom-line, guys please know your boundaries well. For the following points that I am going to make, I will make a quick note now to acknowledge that each women is special, different, and unique in her own right. To break things down simpler for the masses, these are basic and generalized needs that women have.

Women need as much, if not more validation then men. They constantly are under a barrage of pressure to by society to be an act in a certain way. Society puts so much pressure on women to look perfect, and be perfect, that if they don't live up to those standards, it can be tough on them. As her spouse, it is your job to make her feel like she is perfect. Even if her hair is a mess, and she hasn't shaved her legs in a couple of days.

Women are insecure at times as well. Think back to the Taylor Swift song "Mine". Yes I've heard and watched the music video. If you haven't, go watch it and you'll understand what I mean. Oops let's not get sidetracked. Yes please assure your girl that you are going to stick by her side forever, even when things get rough.

Women need to be held too! Cuddling creates endorphins in

the brain that give humans a burst of happiness. These endorphins are drained from a woman's system faster than they are for a man. So she needs to be cuddled more than you realize. If she is having a bad day, suggest she take a break from whatever she is doing and come cuddle with you for fifteen minutes. You would be surprised how much difference such a little break will make.

I don't really want to bring out biology but let's address it head on because, well, why shouldn't we? Now as we all know women go through "that time of the month"; pregnancy, and menopause. *Flashback to a particular Modern Family episode*. These scenarios cause hormonal imbalances in women resulting in discomfort, pain, and mood swings. With that in mind, it is the man's job to be understanding of this. Offer to clean the house for her, or go pick up her favorite meal. This is a way you can show that you love her, and give her what she needs. Offer to pick up any sanitary products she needs. Simple gestures like that make a world of difference to a female. REMEMBER THIS. Also be understanding if she wakes you up at three in the morning to go get her some chicken wings. She can't help it.

Women need to feel protected. They need to feel like nothing in the world is ever going to hurt them ever again. Chances are, she has had a fair share of heartbreak before she met you. Don't break her heart too. Be her superhero, and vow to protect her from evil. Even just saying it while pulling her into a hug will make a huge impact on her. When she feels safe in the relationship, she will open up more and talk about what bothers her, rather than keep it bottled up until she snaps. Chris Daughtry's Song "Superman" would pretty much sum up this whole paragraph. Go take a listen, I'm sure you'll like it.

Women need to feel important in your life. Even if nothing major happened, she needs to feel like she was a part of it. Tell her about your day, give her details of what happened, even if they were boring. Talk about how you missed her while you were at work, and describe an interesting person you saw at work that day.

Women need to be loved. They need romance. This doesn't mean drop a thousand dollars a week on her. It can be small things like planning a picnic, bringing her some flowers that you picked from a field. Cooking dinner for her after she had a long day, or bring her breakfast in bed. She just needs some effort put into it. Even if it doesn't cost a dime. Adam Levine knows this best in "She Will Be Loved".

Now now I get that I'm making a lot of popular culture music references. But hey sometimes music captures very important elements that resonates with us longer in our minds because we listen to them over and over again. We subconsciously absorb the content and unconsciously act on them too. So do find songs that drive home the points that I'm making because I'm sure you'd enjoy listening to them as much as you like reading about them. They are a perfect complement to one another. Am I right or am i right?

Okay so Why again this Key is Important?

You need to understand and truly know your spouse, that way you can anticipate any problems that may arise. You will be in blissful peace if you can use this key to unlock the ability to solve problems before they start. And you will also unlock a compassion rivaled only by that of a small child watching someone cry.

Chapter 3

secret key #2

Be Open Minded

This is the second key you need to own. Most people don't know that marriage is based on being willing to listen to what your partner has to say with an open heart. Over eighty five percent of people say that they would not budge their values to please a spouse. However, sometimes you have to budge a little bit, to unlock the raw emotion in your spouse that you really need to access to be close to them. You should want to know every part of them without judging them, for only then can you reach the depths of their soul that no one else has been to.

Marriage is a whole lot of give and take. There is not much that you can have exactly how you want it. In marriage, you often find out things about the other person that you didn't know when you were dating, and you have to be prepared for this shock. You can't be mad at a person for not showing you everything in the this lovey phase of your relationship with them. They could jolly-well be concealing that side of themselves so as to present to you the best impression that they can give to you. Time will unlock the vulnerable and raw side of your spouse. So give it time and be open about it.

You have to be willing to accept them even after they have told you about themselves, and you have found out things that may not be to pleasant. These things could be as small as them having having a quirky way of eating their food, to major mind-blowing facts like discovering how many partners they have been with prior to marrying you. Remember when you said "I do"? You promised to take your spouse for the good and the bad. So you have to be prepared for anything.

Here are some scenarios in the form of mini fiction stories that should help you understand more what it means to be open minded. These stories are different for the types of families out there whether they have kids or not. There is one scenario for every type of classification of family.

Couples with Kids

Scenario

Stacy had just married her boyfriend of six years two months ago, and the honeymoon phase was just starting to fade. She was shocked that there even was a honeymoon phase to begin with, seeing as she had lived with her husband Josh for five years before they were married, and they had two kids together. She felt that they had already been through everything they could have gone through together. She took a peak into her room to look at her sleeping husband and sighed with happiness. She repeated the action while peeking into her kids rooms. Stacy was happy, and she felt that nothing could spoil her life.

Stacy was far from right with that thought. Later that day, an officer arrived at her door. Stacy was confused, as she didn't have any idea why he would be there. Then she saw another officer standing there holding a baby in a car-seat.

"Josh! Get out here please!" she called down the hallway to her husband's office where he was busy working.

Her kids came out of the room to investigate, but Stacy sent them back. Josh came down the hall and stopped dead in his tracks when he saw the officers and the baby.

"What is going on here?" He asked

The officer that knocked on the door stepped forward, and offered his hand to shake with the couple. They took it and shook it briefly.

"I'm Officer Jennings, and this here is Officer Saul" Officer Jennings gestured to the other officer who was holding the infant, before continuing the conversation. "I'm sure you have a lot of questions, but let me get through explaining the situation to you before you ask, do we have a deal?"

"Yes" Josh and Stacy replied in unison

"Three days ago, a woman by the name of Allisson Marx passed away in childbirth. Doctors told her early on she probably would not survive giving birth, but she decided to go ahead with the pregnancy anyways. She noted the birth father, and ask that he be notified if she did pass. The birth father is noted here as Josh Layman. The same Josh Laymen that is noted to live at this address. She has also left a number for you to call. As you are the father you have to either sign over custody, or claim custody. You have to wait three days to sign over custody however, as this is a long weekend, and all the offices are closed. We are required to give you custody until you are able to make a decision. Now, any questions?"

After Stacy and Josh asked their questions, the officers left, leaving the baby and a few boxes of diapers and formula, along with informing them of the child's name.

" How did this happen?! And don't give me some smart ass answer. I know how this happened, I just want to know when and why!" Stacy asked adamantly.

"Mommy? Can we come out now?" Her oldest son asked.

"Not right now sweetie. Mommy and Daddy are having a

grown up discussion"

"Okay Mommy."

Josh turned to Stacy. I know you are angry. And you have every right to be. But it isn't what you think. I didn't cheat on you. I got with Allisson when we separated over a year ago. I dated her almost the entire five months we were separated. I had no idea she was pregnant though. I know you are probably really angry, but this is my child. I don't want to sign over my rights to her."

Discussion

Stacy has one of two options here. She could force Josh to either give up the baby or lose her and his other kids, or she could be open-minded, and accept this child as her own. Let's talk about the consequences of each action, starting with the first.

If she were to give Josh an ultimatum, he would either sign over the rights to the child he doesn't know and lose the two he does, along with his new wife. He would probably chose to sign over the baby.

If he signed over that child, he would spend the rest of their marriage blaming her, and resenting his other kids, because he never got the chance to know his daughter. This would cause a major rift in their relationship, and could potentially destroy it, and that would leave their marriage the same as it would have been if he refused to sign over the rights.

However, if Stacy is open-minded, she will realize that while her husband had been with another woman, they were not together, and had agreed to see other people at that time, so he really did nothing wrong. She could also have a wonderful addition to her new family, and get to watch another beautiful baby grow up. She could have a daughter along with her two sons, and though that baby girl didn't come from her, she could grow to love that child as much as her biological children.

Being open-minded can save their marriage, and even add to it. Though the child was unexpected, being able to take her in and love her unconditionally will make them stronger as a family, and her compassion will ignite a fire in Josh's heart, which will in turn reignite the flame in hers.

Couples Trying to Have Children

Scenario

Layne and Michal Sherwood had been married for three years before they decided to try to have children. Michal was adamant that he and Layne have only biological children.

He refused to adopt, because he wanted his children to be his and his alone. He didn't want someone else's kids. Michal was excited when Layne said that she was ready to try to have kids. They tried for two years, suffering two miscarriages, before they finally decided to go to a specialist.

"Mr. and Mrs. Sherwood? I am Dr. Branston" an elderly man came in and shook their hands before continuing "I am afraid I have some bad news. We ran several tests, and have confirmed that not only are you ninety percent infertile Mr. Sherwood, but Mrs. Sherwood, you are unable to carry a child full term due to a poorly angled uterus. This is the first case I have had in fifteen years that we couldn't at least use a surrogate in. I am sorry to say that naturally having kids is just not in the cards for you two." and with that the doctor left, and a nurse showed them out of the office.

When they got home, Michal was furious. He never wanted to have to adopt but it seemed that adopting was his only option. His wife wanted a family as well, so he couldn't just think about what he wanted.

Discussion

Now Michal could refuse to adopt, and they could live out their lives without a child, but that is not the life they want to live. They both want children. If Michal refuses to change his mind, he could potentially lose his wife of five years, because he was too stubborn to be open-minded.

However if he chooses to adopt, he can bring a joy and a wonderful passion into his family, and it could bring him and his wife closer, because they will not only have a child, they can bring happiness to a child's life that may not have had that happiness otherwise.

Being open-minded in this scenario can give this couple the family they want, and can bring them closer together, as they tackle an obstacle together.

Couple Without Children

This scenario is completely different, as there are no children involved whatsoever.

Scenario

Scott and Casey have been married for two years. When they started dating, Scott voiced his distaste for tattoos and piercings, and Casey told him that she loved them. He told her that they were gross, and for a while she shoved down her obsession with them to try to make them happy.

One day, Casey decided that she needs to do what makes her

happy, so she goes and gets a tattoo. She had tried to understand why her husband didn't like them, but he could give no other explanation other than they were not natural. She tried being open-minded and seeing things his way, but soon she realized that he had no reason not to like them other than just being judgmental, so she started pressing for a tattoo, and piercings. Her husband forbade her from getting them.

Casey was so angry at being told she was not allowed to do something with her own body that she went and got a tattoo. She decided she was tired of letting her husband control her.

When she got home, her husband was really angry. He yelled at her for hours before finally calming down.

Discussion

Scott has two options here. He can either leave her because she disobeyed a direct order, or he can be open-minded and listen to why she wanted the tattoo in the first place.

If he leaves her over a tattoo, he is throwing away two years of a great marriage because he was too stubborn to realize that his wife was her own person, and in control of her own body. This would be the biggest mistake he ever made, because looks change, but the heart never does, and while his wife had new ink, she was still the same loving person he married.

However, if he actually opens his mind, and decides to listen to why she wanted the tattoos and piercings, and accepts her for who she is, she will love him even more, for making an effort to be loving and accepting of things he didn't like. And maybe, he will eventually come to love her tattoos and piercings, as he loves her. He may even want a few of his own. You never know.

Recap

Those are the three scenarios that could happen, and how to handle them. These are just examples of what could happen. As stated above, every situation is different. If you are open minded, then you can learn more about your partner, and maybe, just maybe, you will find that you actually love these things.

Being open-minded is very important in a marriage, because the willingness to step out of your comfort zone makes it clear that you love that person more than yourself, which only makes them love you more. Passion stems from seeing things that make you fall in love all over again.

Try New Things

Being open minded is not just about being accepting of things that you don't agree with, it is learning to love things that your partner loves. There are a lot of things out there that you may not love, and that is okay, but if your partner loves it, then you should try to show an interest in it.

You and your spouse are two different people, and while you probably have a few common interests, you probably also have some things that you like that aren't shared by your spouse. That is okay. Your spouse probably has things that you don't particularly care for either. However, unless it is an unhealthy habit, you should never tell them they need to quit their hobby. You should always support your spouse to the fullest when they enjoy something.

It is also good to try to learn more about what they enjoy. Ask them to teach you more about what they enjoy, and watch their face light up like a kid on their birthday opening presents. Just knowing that you are trying to enjoy what they enjoy is enough to make them want to take you in their arms and show you how much they love you right then and there.

Showing your partner that you care about what they are doing, and what they enjoy, even if you don't really enjoy those things yourself will make them love you even more, because you are making an effort to join them in their happiest times. Ask them to talk about their passion, and really watch them as they talk about it. Listen to the excitement as they get into explaining something about it, and how much brighter their eyes get as they babble on and on about it. Ask questions, and don't make them ever feel like you are bored. But I guarantee you, that even if their passion is watching grass grow, you will not be bored watching them talk about it. The way they let go, and the raw excitement and happiness on their face will make you fall even more in love with your spouse. You get to see a side of them that few others get to see, and it will make you want to keep them talking for hours.

Trying new things can help your marriage, because your spouse does not have to feel like they have to hide a part of themselves to be with you, and it will be a much happier environment. That happiness will turn into passion, and that passion will lead to more intimacy.

Why You Need This Key

This key is one of the most important keys in this book, because when someone feels that they can come to you without fear of judgment no matter what it is they need (or want) to say, it will create a bond filled with trust, and this will bring you closer together, as you learn more about each other, and allow each other deep within your minds, hearts and souls.

Chapter 4

secret key #3

Make Time for Yourselves

This key is needed to unlock parts of yourself, more than parts of your partner. It unlocks all the honeymoon feelings that you have stored away due to life trying to destroy them. Very few couples realize that time apart and time together apart from everything is needed to really fall in love with your spouse over and over again.

Life gets busy, and sometimes you don't realize that you haven't had any time to yourselves for a while. This section will include how to go about arranging alone time, both with each other, away from the rest of the world, and separate from each other.

Firstly, you need some time together away from the rest of the world. Life gets busy, especially if you are both working, and have conflicting schedules. However, you have to make time for each other, so that you can rekindle that spark every now and then.

Imagine this scenario. The characters will have names but you can substitute your own. Just relax and put yourself in this scene.

Scenario

Jillian smiled across the table at her husband. Tonight was the first night in over three years that they had been out on a date together. Between work, carpool, taking care of the kids, and just a plain busy life, they had not been able to enjoy each other's company for quite some time. That was until Alex, her wonderful husband, had set up this surprise.

Alex knew that his wife needed a break, so he figured what better time to do it, than over the long weekend? He kept the entire thing a secret, making sure that their two boys never said a word about spending a few days with their Uncle Ted. He set up reservations at a hotel so that his wife would not be tempted to use the quiet time to clean house. He got a table at a different nice restaurant for dinner all three nights. He had everything planned out, and it was being executed perfectly.

"How is dinner, my love?" Alex asked Jillian.

"It is wonderful, Dear." Jillian sighed with contentment.

Alex stared with wonder at his beautiful bride, and found himself falling in love with her all over again. She had forgone her usual bun for an elaborate up-do, and she had traded her usual old t-shirt and yoga pants for the red satin dress that had sat unworn in the closet for years. It still fit her as well as it did the last time she wore hit. His mind instantly went back to that night, and the passion that filled it. Almost four years ago, the night they conceived their youngest son. His trousers started to tighten at the thought of reliving that passion this weekend.

Jillian looked up and noticed her husband's eyes blazing with desire as he looked at her. She blushed. It had been awhile since he looked at her that way. Or maybe he had, and she just never noticed. But she had a feeling it had something to do with the fact that she wasn't in her usual housewife attire.

Jillian took some time to admire her husband as well. Instead of the sawdust covered t-shirt, dirty old work jeans, and scuffed boots, her husband had donned a three-piece suit she hadn't seen in a while. She admired the way it contoured against his body, showing off the muscles he had gained since starting his new job at a construction site. The pants cupped his rear quite nicely as well. She can't remember the last time he looked this fit. Not even the night that they conceived their youngest son, the most passion that they had ever seen in their marriage, the last time he wore that suit. She felt herself getting hot and flustered as she began to daydream herself back to that day.

"You look stunning tonight, baby." Alex said, breaking her reverie.

" As do you, darling" Jillian replied, smiling at Alex again.

They finished dinner, and went back to the hotel. They weren't quite ready to go in yet, so they walked through the hotel garden under the light of the full moon. Alex slid his arm around his wife's waist, and pulled her close to him. He couldn't stand not being able to see her face though, so he pulled her in front of him. Their bodies pressed together in the moonlight, he stared into her gorgeous blue-green eyes, and noted how rosy her cheeks were. Even though she wore only the slightest hint of makeup, her features were striking, and he wondered why he hadn't noticed how beautiful she had become since the birth of their last child. His wife had always been beautiful, but lately, Jillian had been working out to lose some of that stubborn baby weight. As sad as he was to see it go, he couldn't help but see how much happier she was with how she looked, and tonight it shined through.

Her happy face was the most beautiful thing he had ever seen, and he would do anything to keep that smile on her face. He leaned in for a kiss, and watched as her gorgeous eyes fluttered shut. Her long dark lashes cast half-moon shadows on her cheeks, and her perfect heart-shaped lips parted as she awaited the feel of his lips on hers. He kissed her softly, and felt the passion between them build. Their kiss ignited like a white hot fire, and he knew he needed to have her. Now. With deep regret, he pulled away from their kiss, and grabbed her hand as they ran back to the hotel. They were barely in the door, when she shoved him up against the door, and their lips met again, barely parting at all as they removed each other's clothes on the way to the bedroom.

Discussion

Jillian and Alex rekindled a passion that they haven't felt in three years. All it took was some time away from the world, for them to find the passion that the were missing in their lives. They fell in love again within a few hours of being alone, and they remembered why they got married in the first place.

Spending some time together away from everyone else is essential in a marriage. You have to have some time to really enjoy each other, or else you will begin to forget why you fell in love with each other. The daily routines you both have that take you in different directions put a lot of strain on your marriage, and if you go too long without having some time together, you begin to feel like strangers. You cannot function in a marriage if you feel that you do not know the person sleeping next to you.

There is also the matter of spending alone time by yourselves. You need some time to be you without anyone else. Some time to unwind and refresh. This may mean you take a hike for a few hours, or you go out to the club without your spouse or mutual friends. Maybe you curl up with a good book, and enjoy some peace and quiet. In this scenario, you will find how important some alone time really is.

Rachel was sitting on the greyhound looking out the window. She had been traveling for three days, trying to get back home. She left her husband in California, and was heading back home to Florida. As she sat on the bus she had a lot of time to think.

Juan was a loving husband, they were together all of the time, and everyone thought that their marriage was perfect, but the past several months they had been fighting constantly. They argued over every little thing. Their last argument, Juan got violent with her. He shoved her into the wall on the staircase landing, and then tripped her down the stairs. He had never been violent with her before, but she wasn't going to stand for it at all. In the middle of the night, she cleaned out her bank account, and bought a bus ticket home. She took nothing but a suitcase and a carry-on, and their six month old daughter.

She thought back to when things were great. That was before Juan lost his job, and she had to get a job. She found a job working from home for good pay, so that she was able to stay home due to being very pregnant. After Olivia was born, things started to go south. Juan refused to get up in the middle of the night with their daughter, and became very lazy. This caused fights. Rachel was stressed to the max with a newborn, a demanding job, and a husband who wouldn't step up to help. They fought more and more, until one day everything fell apart.

Now Rachel was sitting on a bus, her daughter in a carrier in the seat beside her, and she wonders if she did the right thing. There is never any excuse for violence in a relationship, but in their three years together that was the first instance of any violence, and he was horrified with himself after-wards.

Discussion

Juan and Rachel fought because they never had any time apart. Juan slept so much just to get some space from his wife, and thus he missed out on the time period needed to help his wife. The fights got worse, and Juan became more and more agitated, mostly at himself for not being able to find a new job, and one day he snapped.

While there is no excuse to get violent in a relationship, this could have been avoided if they had taken some time for themselves, rather than spend every waking moment together. The fights also could have been avoided if Juan had stepped up and helped with Olivia and the household, but that falls more under communication and understanding.

You need space in a relationship. Not only from the world, but from each other as well. You need to miss each other, and you need to have that time where you aren't working or taking care of kids, but you still have your space from each other as well. Just as you need regular date nights. Even if it is something inexpensive, you still need to take that time to rekindle the flame.

So no matter how busy your schedule is, make some time to find yourself, and to rediscover your partner. No job, carpool, or dance recital is worth losing your marriage. And that isn't to say that kids aren't important, you just can't spend every single moment of your lives doting on them.

Go Out with Friends

You don't just need time alone and time apart, you also need friends outside of your children. (If you have children.) You need time away. Don't let anyone tell you that you are a bad parent because you need time away from your kids a couple nights a month, whether it be to unwind together, separate, or with friends. You are humans, and you deserve some space as well. You can't be expected to be a superhero, and be with your children all the time. They need to learn what it is like to be apart from you sometimes so that they don't develop separation anxiety. As long as you are not going out every weekend, there is no harm in some alone time. Go out. Have fun. Be free. Don't let anyone make you feel bad for being human.

Find some friends to go out to the bar with. Find some friends to go hiking with. Find friends that have common interests. Just find some people that you can go out with. They can have children or be child free, depending on the type of conversation you want to have. If you want a conversation that doesn't always steer towards kids, child free friends would be the way to go.

Bottom line of this chapter is: You are human, and need some time away from the world. You need to have fun, and unwind. Don't be afraid to act like a human, just because you are married doesn't mean the fun has to end.

Why You Need this Key

This key is instrumental in unlocking your old feelings for your partner. Back to the days where the passion ran wild, and your hearts were free from stress and sadness. Couples need this key if they want to feel like young lovers again.

Chapter 5

secret key #4

Intimacy

This is the chapter that may not be for some people, however, if you want your marriage to succeed and succeed extraordinarily, reading this chapter is imperative. Put your discomfort aside, and you may find you enjoy this chapter, along with some useful information to aid you in your marriage.

Make a Sex List

According to research, couples that have regular sex are 75% more likely to have a successful marriage than couples who do not. Couples who are adventurous with sex are also 18% more likely to have a successful marriage than even those who have regular sex. This key is necessary to unlock the carnal parts of yourself and your partner that have never been touched before.

Sex is important in a marriage. Plain and simple. Not only is it used for procreation, it is a pleasurable bonding experience between you and your partner. However, it needs to go beyond the missionary stage eventually.

Think about the last time you had sex. Were you into it? Or did you just do it because you had the time, and you weren't sure when you would have the time again? Was it interesting? Or boring? If it felt forced and boring, it could be that you need to step out of your normal sex routine. This chapter will go over what goes into making sex fun and enjoyable for both parties, and what types of sex there are. Lastly, this chapter will go over how to make a sex list and what exactly you use a sex list for.

Enjoying Sex

It is important to enjoy sex with your partner. It should not feel forced, it should feel like a loving, passionate experience every time. Even if you are just having a quickie in the laundry room while your kids are downstairs watching television and waiting for their dinosaur nuggets to come out of the oven. It should feel like a dirty little secret that makes you blush every time you think of it, yet still gives you butterflies that make you want to do it again. The passion in your love making should rival that of the passion in a steamy adult novel.

This is achieved by several steps. You can't just throw in a new position, and expect sex to feel phenomenal. It may be a little better, but there is more to sex than just the act itself. You have to mentally be in the zone as well as physically.

Foreplay

Foreplay is more than just a little kissing and oral sex. It is the time before sex that you use to clear your mind of everything but sex and breathing. You can't just kiss a few places and call it good. The best foreplay starts hours before the sex. Here are a few things you can do to make foreplay a part of your life.

FOREPLAY AT WORK-

Yes, that is correct. You can start foreplay even while both you and your partner are at work. On your breaks, and your lunch, text your partner all the things you want to do that night. Be descriptive and be forward. Don't beat around the bush making things confusing for your partner to figure out. The brashness of your texts will catch them off guard, and really turn them on. This is where you have to be careful though. Make sure you only text them on your breaks. You don't want to get in trouble from your boss because you are texting at work. Also, the added anticipation of getting to text them again makes the moment build.

Once you get home, the foreplay doesn't stop there. As you go about your daily chores, add in a few inappropriate touches here and there. Grab your partner's rear end, crotch or (if female), chest as you are walking by. These little naughty touches will leave you wanting more.

After dinner, and putting the kids to bed, if you have kids, take a shower together. Wash each other all over, taking explicit pleasure in the genital areas, and use the soap to stimulate your partner, and have them do the same. You can actually initiate sex in the shower as well if you wish, but sometimes it is nice to just keep the foreplay there.

Once you move to the bedroom, this is where you can start the in-depth foreplay, and move onto the heavy making out, and heavy petting. Start out slow, and gently. Do not move too fast, as you want to make the moment last. Slowly move from heavy petting to oral.

Once you both reach your first orgasm, this is when to start the actual sex part begins. If your spouse is male, and has a hard time getting it up after an orgasm, there is a trick to make him orgasm without ejaculating, as ejaculation is what releases all the hormones.

To do this, he has to be vocal about how close he is, and you have to find the right spot. Right behind his testicles, where they meet the perineum (area that connects the penis to the rectum), is a hard spot about the size of a nickel. Right as he is about to ejaculate, you have to press hard on that spot, rubbing in circular motions. This will stop the ejaculation process, while still allowing him to feel the pleasure of an orgasm. It takes a few times to get this down, as you have to find the PC muscle and hit it at just the right time while continuing to stimulate him, but once you get it down, he can have multiple orgasms with no refractory time.

It is a lot easier for a female to have multiple orgasms if she is truly mentally present. For a female to have multiple orgasms though, or for her to even achieve one, she has to focus on how the sex feels. Ladies, you can't think about the milk in the fridge, and wonder if it is going to expire soon. You can't worry about if someone is going to hear you. You have to be selfish. Ask for what you want, and let yourself be free to feel the great feelings of sex. Don't try to put on an act, and don't worry about impressing your partner. I can assure you that seeing you enjoy yourself will be sexy enough for them. Just enjoy yourself in the raw moment.

A lot of experts say to fake it until you make it. This is great in theory, except you get so focused on faking it that you will never make it. You have to let it happen naturally. Otherwise you will be left disappointed every time.

Sex Positions

I bet right now you are trying to think of all the sex positions you can. Of course there is the standard ones such as missionary, doggy style, and cowgirl, but there are a few more that you should be aware of, and these ones are great sex positions to rock your world.

- The Cat: This position is great for allowing a female to achieve orgasm. It provides both penetration and clitoral stimulation. It is set up like the missionary, female on bottom, male on top. However, the males chest is above the females shoulders, and the females hips are raised. The male should grind rather than thrust for optimal pleasure.

- Waterfall: This is great for male orgasm. The setup is like the cowgirl, but the male hangs off of the bed with his head touching the floor, and his pelvis on the bed. Be careful not to be to rough with this position to avoid spinal injury.
- The Hot Seat: This is another good one for female orgasm, and as a plus, it puts her in control. Sit on a chair, or the edge of the bed, with your feet on the floor. Have her sit on your lap, and slide yourself into her. She can control the angle and depth by leaning forward, or arching her back. You can also add variations of this by sitting on a washer or dryer on the highest agitation cycle, or on the staircase.
- Reverse Cowgirl: This is good for both partners to orgasm. It is exactly what the title states, the cowgirl with the female the opposite way.
- Pole Position: This one offers a great view for the guys, and great stimulation for the female. The male should lay on his back with one leg bent while the other is out

straight. The female should straddle the raised leg, and slide onto the male's penis. The female gets penetration stimulation from the penis, and clitoral stimulation from the raised thigh.

- The Lap Dance: This one is great for intimacy. The male sits on the edge of the bed, and the female straddles him face to face. This is great for making out while having sex.
- The Anvil: This one is a very pleasurable technique. The female lies on her back, and the male kneels between her legs, resting the calves on his shoulders. This angle allows for deep penetration, and g-spot stimulation.
- Those are some of the sex positions that will rock your worlds. Try out as many as you would like, and if you want you can even try to make up your own, or look up more online.

-

- **What is a Sex List**
- A sex list is literally what it says. A list of sex positions. You fill it up with positions you would like to try, along with styles you would like to try. BDSM, Pegging, Three-ways, etc. Don't be afraid that your partner will think you are weird, he or she probably has some weird stuff on their list

- Agree to a time line to finish your list by. This could be in days, weeks, or even years. I would suggest that you stretch it out for as long as possible, that way you have something to look forward to.
- **How to Make a Sex List**
- It is fairly simple. Look through all the kinds of sex positions, and sex styles you would like to try, and then write them down on the list. You and your partner should be open-minded to everything the other puts down, and you should vow to at least try everything each other has on their list at least once.
- If there is something that you absolutely do not want to do, and can give a valid reason as to why, rather than "it just seems weird" then your partner should scratch it off the list. You should do the same for them if it is something they cannot do.
- Sex is essential in a marriage, but not just plain sex. Sex that brings you closer together as you try new things and branch out. Sex is needed to procreate, and to ignite passion in your marriage.
-
- **Why this Key is Important**

- This key allows you to tap into your wild side, and be free with the person you most love. They get to see a side of you that no one else has, and that will allow you to build up a passion you have never felt before. By unlocking the beasts inside of yourselves, you can really connect with your partner.

-
-

- Chapter 6
-
- secret key #5

-

- **Find a Common Interest.**

-

- It is true what they say. People that play together stay together. This key unlocks the part of your brain that forms strong bonds with people, and this is necessary to unlock so that you can truly feel at home with the one you love. You need to form a bond that you have never experienced with anyone else in order to be truly happy with your partner.

This will keep you in love with them for the rest of your lives.

-

- While it may have been a common interest that brought you together, you probably have more different hobbies than you have hobbies together. You need common interests so that you have things to do together when you get alone time, and you don't spend that time in a constant barrage of "what do you want to do?" "I don't know, what do you want to do?" back and forth. This is almost as bad as trying to figure out where you want to go when you go out to eat.

- So to avoid the boredom in each other's company, you should go explore some things together, and find some things that you enjoy doing together. There are many things you can do to find out what you like.

  - Join a book club: If both you and your partner love to read, maybe a book club could be just what you need. You can discuss the meeting at home, and trade insight on the book you are reading. You can find time to read books together, and even read excerpts from the book out loud to your children. With a book club, you also get to meet other people with similar interests.

- Take Dance Classes: This is something to do to discover if either of you like dancing. It is always good to know a few basic dances anyhow. When taking dance classes remember, it will take you a bit to learn if you like them or not, because you won't get the dances the first day.

- Go Hiking: Hiking is a great form of exercise, and a great way to bond with your partner. You can go hiking on a trail, and look at all sorts of scenery, and learn about nature, which is one of the most beautiful things in the world. The serenity will give you both peace of mind, and the exercise will keep you fit.

- Take a Shop Class: Learn about wood work or metal work. It is always wonderful to be able to create a work of art with your partner, and it is even better when it is functional.

- There are many other things you can try to find a common interest. Try a new one every month until you find one that works for you. Because when you have something to talk about, then everything else flows easily after.

- Go On Adventures

- These adventures do not have to cost a lot of money. They just have to be something out of your usual routine. Go to your local park, and enjoy the scenery. Visit your local zoo, and see all the animals that are there. Go to the lake and go fishing or boating. It doesn't have to cost a lot, it just has to make a difference.

- The best thing is, you can take your kids if you have them on these adventures. You can be together as a family, and teach your children new things. It is amazing the impact it has on your life, how much difference an afternoon out makes.

- This next scenario will show you just how much different things can be before and after an adventure.

- Scenario

- Alice and Walker had been fighting a lot recently. Literally all the time. Alice had recently found out that Walker had cheated on her with her ex best friend. She was furious, but didn't want to leave because she loved Walker, and they had three children together. She didn't want to split her family up.

- So for the past two months of her life, she has been living in a miserable hell. Walker tried to act like nothing had happened, and didn't even try to apologize for hurting her like he did. He merely admitted that he made a mistake and it won't happen again, and left it at that. However, Alice's trust for him was completely shattered, and her heart was broken. That pain turned into anger most of the time, and Alice started fights over little things, or got irrationally angry. These fights could start at the drop of a hat, and last for hours. It was hell on Earth in that household. Till one day, their oldest daughter came out into the living room and said four words that changed their perspective.

- "I hate living here" Macy said with tears in her eyes
- "Oh baby girl, what's wrong?" Alicia asked
- "Ever since Daddy hurt you, all you two do is fight. I wish Daddy would just leave. I hate seeing you unhappy Mommy."
- "Don't you love me anymore, Mace?" Walker asked
- "Of course I love you Daddy. You just hurt Mommy, and you should be punished. When it happens on TV, the mom kicks the dad out, and the dad only gets to visit. It teaches him a good lesson."
- "Oh, Macy. That is TV. In real life, it isn't that easy. I love your father very much, and do not want him to leave. Things are just rough right now. My heart has an injury on it, like when you scrape your knee. And it is going to hurt until it heals. I know I shouldn't be so crabby, it is just hard sometimes." Alice explained.
- "Alice, Macy, go get the other two, and pack a picnic

lunch. I have an idea." Walter suddenly said.

- "Where are we going?' Alice asked
- "It's a surprise."
- Twenty minutes later, Walker, Alice, and the kids pulled into a beautiful field with a large pond. The sun on the water was amazing, and there were ducks and geese resting on the water. Armed with fishing poles, bait, bread crumbs, and a picnic basket filled with goodies, the family set out towards the pond.
- "Oh my goodness. The spot where we had out first date, and you taught me how to fish!" Alice exclaimed.
- "I figured we needed to go back to where it all began, to see how far we have come. Six years, and three beautiful children later." Walker stated, with tears in his eyes, as he watched his kids feed the ducks and geese. "I can't believe that Mace wants me gone. I really screwed up this time."
- This was the closest that Walker had come to apologizing for his actions, and Alice felt her heart swell, as she saw for the first time, the regret on his face when he realized what he had done did indeed have some severe implications.
- Throughout the day, Walker and Alice rekindled their flame as they taught their kids how to fish, went swimming in the pond, had a picnic on the dock, and lay back that

evening and watched the sunset. For the first time in two months, their day was filled with laughter, rather than tears and yelling.

- "I'm so sorry, Alice. I know I have never said it, I just couldn't bring myself to admit that my choice had any real effect on you. Even though I saw you hurting every day, it was easier to blame you than to admit I was the one with the problem. I am so sorry. Please, please, please forgive me." Walker apologized.
- "Walker that is the first time you have said you are sorry about this whole thing. That's is what I needed to hear. Yes I forgive you. I love you with all my heart. Can you forgive me for picking useless fights?"
- "Alice, without those useless fights, I could have lost you and the kids. Those fights were you fighting for us, and I could never be mad at you for that." Walker pulled her up, and put their song playing on his phone, and he danced with her, as their children watched. Alice's heart swelled as she remembered this was the song they danced too on their very first date, in that very same spot.
- "I knew then that you were the only one for me, and though I messed up and almost forgot that fact, I am even more sure now."

- For the first time since she found out about the infidelity, Alice kissed him. Not a peck on the lips kind of kiss. She gave him one of those every day when he left for work. A deep, passionate kiss, filled with love and desire.
- Once the kiss ended, Walker got down on one knee and pulled out her engagement ring, which she had taken off the day she learned of his transgressions.
- "I know I messed up, and I want to do it better this time around. Alice, I love you with all of my heart. I never want to hurt you like that again. I have truly learned my lesson, and I want to have another chance to become the man you deserve in your life. Will you marry me?"
- "Yes." Alice whispered, tears falling down her cheeks. In that moment she was the happiest she had been in months.
- Their children cheered, and were ecstatic to see their parents happy again. They finished the night out with stargazing, and a healing family.
- Discussion
- Alice and Walker's marriage was severely on the rocks after Walker's infidelity was brought to life. It seemed like things would never get better, but after a wake-up call, and a little family adventure, Alice and Walker were on the path to setting things right again. It won't be perfect over night,

but with a little work, a rocky marriage can be fixed.

- Those are the five secret keys to a successful, passionate, and intimate relationship. Read on for more info on tips and tricks to know what to expect, and if your marriage is just on the rocks, or if it is dangerous.

-

- **Why You Need This Key**
- To truly be in love with someone, you need to experience something together, that you haven't with anyone else. Finding a common interest or going on adventures will unlock that experience for you so that you can truly feel each other deep down in your souls.

CHAPTER 7

Extra help for those in a vulnerable place

Is it Rocky? Or Dangerous?

I included this chapter to address a common phenomenon that I realized is commonly overlooked by most. That is how to recognize a rocky marriage versus a potentially abusive and dangerous one. It is vital that you understand the difference so that you are able to discern a healthy versus a toxic marriage. Healthy marriages can be fixed. Toxic marriages will need a large clean-up crew to fix the massive oil-spill. And as we know, the existing toxicity has already begun destroying the beauty that it had infected. Be alert to the warning signs please. Here we go.

A rocky marriage can be fixed with a little understanding. If you are fighting over simple things that can be changed but you want some expert advice by a health professional to breathe new insights into the source of the problems between you and your spouse, seeing a marriage counselor might be an excellent idea. The counselor can help you and your spouse delve deeper into the underlying issues of the marriage and to work towards a healthy resolution.

- However, if your partner is always picking fights based on things you can't change, like your appearance, your voice, your shoe size, or even how you breathe. Say What? Well if they are constantly make you feel insecure, it could be indication that there is some deeper issues with the relationship that might not be so easily solved. Now if it gets violent, that's when you NEED help. Also i might classify some of the above mentions as abuse. Abuse you say? Yes abuse.

- Abuse isn't always physical, though that is a part of it. Abuse can take the form where they make you feel so low about yourself that you want to end it all to make your life easier. Or if they make you feel trapped in your marriage, and tell you they are the only person who will ever love you, and that you should be grateful they put up with you. Generally this is the behavior of a narcissist. Do not allow this to continue. Tell them how they make you feel, and if they are willing to try to change, it is okay to give them one more chance, as long as they actively get professional help. However, if they continue to belittle your feelings and you realize they can never change, it is time to think long and hard whether you would want to be spending the rest of your life with such a person. Get a second opinion from your friends and loved ones. Make an informed decision and act on it fast. I firmly believe that this type of treatment is absolutely unacceptable, unhealthy for the abused, and belongs nowhere in a marriage.

- Remember, if they hit you. They will more than likely do it again. This goes for both men and women. Either gender can be the victim, either gender can be the perpetrator. No matter your gender, you should never feel bad about getting help. There are many different resources out there you can reach out to. The best one is http://www.ncadv.org/learn-more/get-help. It gives you a list of places that will help you out, and gives you tips for staying safe.

- Be safe, and remember, just because you say "I do" does not mean that you have to stay with your abuser.

●

●

-
-
-
-
-
-
-
-
-
-
-
-
- conclusion
-

- Thank you again for purchasing this book! I hope this book was able to help you to get closer to your man and to engage in a FIERY relationship with him as well. Go practice and master all that was taught in this book and start creating an ember that turns into a raging fire. Captivate your man, strengthen the relationship, and keep it lasting for as long as there is commitment.

- I wish you all the best in your endeavors and I hope to see you succeed in your relationship now and in the future.

-
-

-

-

-

-

-

-

-

- Thank You and Good Luck!

www.ingramcontent.com/pod-product-compliance
Lightning Source LLC
LaVergne TN
LVHW010314070526
838199LV00065B/5559